CONCILIUM

Religion in the Seventies

CONCILIUM

Religion in the Seventies

Volume 74: Ecumenism

THE PLURALITY
OF MINISTRIES

Edited by
Hans Kung
and Walter Kasper

Herder and Herder

1972
HERDER AND HERDER NEW YORK
232 Madison Avenue, New York 10016

CONTENTS

Editorial

AN ecumenical discussion of the question of office and the mutual recognition of office seems to many to be an unnecessary waste of time. Is it not more important, they say, to think about the life and message of the Church than to concern oneself with church structures, which seem to many people in any case to be outmoded? Should not our first concern today be for the common witness of Christians and churches in the service of peace, for social and racial justice, for the freedom of man and the battle against exploitation and oppression? Do not excessive introversion, arguments about internal structure, and the disagreeable question of office prevent the Church today from turning to the real problems of the human race and—perhaps—even recognizing its opportunity at the present time? And, on the other hand, is not the question of the oneness of the Church first and foremost a question of the common possession of the essence of the Gospel, of common faith in the saving act of Jesus Christ which gives men hope—and only secondarily or not at all a question of common structures in the Church? It is not at all easy to explain why the question of office has latterly moved so much to the forefront of ecumenical interest. At the time of the Reformation it was not the structures of the Church but the essence, the thing itself, the Gospel of Jesus Christ in its sole and universal aspect of salvation (doctrine of justification), that was primary.

These questions have their force. They compel us to justify

7

our concern with the problems of office and the mutual recognition of office.

The question of office is being raised just now in many different forms. The inter-church problem of mutual recognition of office is only one aspect of a very complex situation which expresses itself inside the churches in, for example, a crisis of authority among lay people, and a crisis of identity among the clergy. This is having its effect in a catastrophic decline in vocations. The subject-matter of this issue thus forms part of the larger context of social break-up, the consequences of which cannot yet be gauged, and of a profound crisis in the understanding of authority as it has existed up to now. It is significant that, despite their different traditional and doctrinal understandings of office, all the churches now see themselves as confronted by similar problems. All are being questioned in the same way about their understanding of authority and office. We must not of course overlook the opportunities provided by this and by the revolt of the younger generation for a closer approach of the churches to one another in theological understanding. To come to a new understanding of authority and office in the spirit of the Gospel is for all of them a matter of life and death.

Questions of office and the authority of office are clearly not central to the Gospel. The teaching on office has only a supporting role. The real foundation of the Church and its unity is Jesus Christ and nothing else. All the churches are agreed today that office in the Church can only be understood as service of the Gospel and therefore of men. For this reason it is all the more unendurable for the churches to be in far-reaching agreement on the basic contents of the Gospel (the teaching on justification is hardly a divisive problem any longer), and yet in disagreement about the structural aspects of its witness. If the office is the sign of the Gospel, then the actual teaching about office, and its actualizations, are the signs of a correct or incorrect understanding of the Gospel. The question of the mutual recognition of office thus turns into a test of the extent of common understanding of the essence of the Gospel. This test is all the more essential since complete oneness of the churches is only reached when they are one in common celebration of the Lord's Supper. This oneness, however, always falls short of agreement

about the unresolved question of office. The churches' separation at the Lord's Supper must be all the more painful for them
in view of their growing oneness in mutual witness of love. So
long as this division persists in the centre of Christian and church
life, there can be no truly valid witness to the world outside of
the oneness of the Church. Thus the question of the mutual recognition of office is unavoidable.

J. McKenzie's contribution deals with the plurality of offices
in the New Testament and what this suggests for a Church
divided on this question. The final answer cannot be a single
monolithic ecclesiastical structure but only the mutual recognition of a variety of offices. Such a recognition does of course
presuppose a certain measure of agreement. This brings us to
the task of re-thinking the mutually exclusive elements in the
various confessional traditions. Without such a removal of obstacles from the past, we are not truly free for the future. The
contributions of H. McSorley, J. Zizioulas, J. von Allmen, J. Lescrauwaet and H. Legrand are intended to further this task. But
they can only deal with part of the outstanding problems. The
important question of apostolic succession is omitted here, since
an earlier issue (April 1968) was entirely devoted to it.

Ecumenical theology must be forward-looking today. For
this reason B. Bobrinskoy, U. Kühn, A. Outler, M. Sheperd,
F. Littell and M. Villain try to explain, each from the standpoint
of his own tradition, how we can arrive at mutual recognition
of our respective offices in theology and in practice. The docu-
mentation will show how far talks between the churches have
gone in this respect, and which questions are still outstanding.

This issue would not have been possible without the co-operation of very many people, in particular the writers of the individual articles, some of whom stepped in at the last moment;
and the members of the editorial board, who gave rich and valuable encouragement to the form taken by the argument. They
all deserve our gratitude.

WALTER KASPER

PART I
ARTICLES

John McKenzie

Ministerial Structures in the
New Testament

THE answer of the New Testament to the question of the plurality of ministerial structures is oracular in the sense that it is obscure and ambiguous. To begin with the Roman Catholic structure, no major Roman Catholic ministerial office in its modern form can be found in the New Testament—pope, bishop or priest. For pope and priest the New Testament does not even have the words. The efforts of the Reformers to restore New Testament ministerial offices were ultimately successful. A colleague of a church which shall not be named once remarked to me that it is no easier to find a Stated Clerk in the New Testament than it is to find a Roman Pontiff. If all the Christian churches have evolved their ministerial structures and offices with almost serene indifference to the New Testament, one may ask why the New Testament should be pertinent now. One may further observe that the Christian churches, in determining their structures and offices by the necessities which history and the evolution of culture impose, have been more faithful to the mandate of proclaiming the Gospel than they would have been by mummifying archaic structures. The student of the New Testament first notices that no structure or office is imposed for all times and all places.

The student next notices that church offices in the New Testament cannot be enumerated and can be only vaguely defined. Modern Catholic and Protestant churches have generally uniform ministerial structures; the member of any Christian church has little difficulty recognizing titles and functions in his church anywhere in the world. The Catholic, for example, expects to find and does find bishops and priests everywhere. The American Catholic is bewildered when he first encounters cathedral canons, but when the title is explained to him he has no difficulty locating it within the structure he knows. He will not find the title of priest used in the New Testament; and if he thinks of the New Testament titles of bishop and deacon as he knows these titles, he misunderstands the New Testament. In fact we do not know the function of those men who appear in the New Testament as bishops (overseers), presbyters (elders) and deacons. Still less can we define the titles found in the lists of 1 Cor. 12. 28 and Eph. 4. 11.

I. The Apostolic Ministry

That New Testament office which is best known is the apostolate; and the apostolate 'has not endured beyond the first generation of the Church. The claim of the Catholic episcopacy to be the successors of the apostles has never been understood to mean that the bishops are apostles. Theologians have long agreed that the New Testament texts permit us to define the apostles as those who were witnesses of the resurrection of Jesus and who received a personal commission from Jesus to proclaim the Gospel.[1] Plainly neither the ocular "witness" of the resurrection nor the personal commission from Jesus could endure after the first generation. That office which succeeds the apostolate can include no more than the preservation of the testimony of the immediate witnesses of the resurrection and the proclamation of the Gospel by a commission from some other than Jesus. The New Testament, unlike modern canon law, is by no means clear on the identity of the authority which commissions the preaching.

This definition of apostle is broader than the Twelve of the New Testament. Most of what is known about the apostolic office is derived from the Pauline writings, and Paul was not one of the Twelve. His commission was a personal commission from the risen Jesus; and he affirms not only that his commission was authentic, but also that he had received "the apostolate of the

[1] K. H. Rengstorf in Kittel ThWBNT I, 423.

Gentiles", as Peter had received the apostolate of the Jews (Gal 2. 7–9). Such a commission to Peter is not reported in the gospels, all of which are later compositions than Gal. The two commissions would seem very nearly to cover all the territory there was, and to leave nothing for the rest of the Twelve, or for those others like Barnabas who had the title of apostle. In fact, however, Peter's commission was understood of the Jews of the Diaspora, and this leaves room for the remarkable and un-explained position of James in the Jesusalem church.

In spite of Paul's claim to a personal commission from Jesus, his first mission, according to Acts 13. 1–3, came to him through what we are tempted to call canonical channels. He and Barnabas were selected by a charismatic inspiration of the "prophets and teachers" of Antioch for the mission to the Gentiles. Who were these prophets and teachers, whose names are given? And who founded the church of Antioch? The names are not given (Acts 11. 19–21). Possibly the most momentous decision of the infant Church was made by men whose office and authority we are unable to define. Here we may encounter some of the free narra-tive which is distressingly frequent in Luke. Paul, for instance, never acknowledges the "church" of Antioch as his "superior"; he acknowledges no superior, and he explicitly rejects any auth-ority claimed over him by the "church" of Jerusalem. I place the word "church" in quotation marks because it is impossible to define the office which could be alleged to exercise control over the proclamation of the Gospel. In fact no office with such control appears.

The work of the apostle, as it is seen in Paul, can be summed up in modern terms as preaching and organizing. It was a point of pride with Paul that he preached only where no one had preached before him (Rom. 15. 20–21; 2 Cor. 10. 14–16). It may have been a point of procedure also, but we cannot reconstruct the procedures of the apostolic Church. "Preaching" is not the most felicitous rendition of the Greek word *kerygma*, which con-temporary theologians have given an importance it has not always had. Were it not for such passages as 1 Cor. 15. 3–5 and the sermons of Acts 2–13 studied by C. H. Dodd,[2] we would know

[2] C. H. Dodd, *The Apostolic Preaching and its Development* (1936).

little of what the apostle said when he proclaimed the good news. As an organizer the apostle is no better known. To take Corinth as an example, Paul spent eighteen months there and left a church completely organized and independent of any other church and of himself. Of the ministerial structure of the church of Corinth the epistles tell us nothing. We can conclude from none of the epistles that the ministerial structure of the Pauline churches was uniform. We can conclude with no more certainty about the structures of churches founded by others than Paul; and it must be added that we know nothing of the identity of the "founders" of such celebrated churches as the churches of Rome, Alexandria and, as we have already mentioned, Antioch.

II. The Governing of the Community

In the modern Church it may seem paradoxical, not to say highly questionable, to point out that one thing the New Testament apostle does not do and has no commission to do is govern the Church. The letters of Paul are not fragments of a vast but lost collection of documents of administration by correspondence. Paul had what he thought were more important things to do. The letters suggest that Paul wrote when he was written to, or that he responded to an interest of Christian friendship. The "business" of Corinth and Philippi, whatever that business normally was, was conducted by the churches of Corinth and Philippi, more precisely by officers whom we know as "bishops", "presbyters" and "deacons"; we cannot define their functions precisely, and we cannot even define how many of them would be found in a single church. If Corinth wished to send preachers to some city which had not been evangelized, they were free to do it, as far as we know. They might have regarded this as a religious re-enactment of the earlier Greek practice of colonization.

There is no clear commission given to anyone to "govern" the New Testament Church. The exegesis which found the power of jurisdiction in the rock and the keys of the kingdom does not even reach the level of midrashic. The metaphor of the shepherd was indeed an ancient Oriental metaphor of royal power, found as far back as Egyptian monumental sculpture and the laws of

Hammurabi. But in the Gospel of John the figure is dominated by the image of Jesus, the good shepherd who gives his life for his sheep (John 10. 1–18). Those who have the first place in the Church are instructed to be the *diakonos* of others (Mark 10. 42–45; Matt. 20. 25–28; Luke 22. 24–27). In the world in which this saying was formed the *diakonos* did not rule the household. The New Testament does not think of government as a form of "ministry", the word which comes from the Latin *ministerium* and the Greek *diakonia*. Those who have wished to form structures of church government have had to do it without using the New Testament—except by mistranslating it. The structure of decision in the New Testament is not so much monarchic or democratic as unformed and unsophisticated. The only major decision described in the New Testament (Acts 15. 1–29) may not have happened as Luke describes it,[3] but the narrative must represent a procedure known to Luke from experience. The decision was reached by an assembly whose components cannot be identified; the "apostles" in Luke's use of the title probably are the Twelve, but the *presbyteroi* can signify all the adult male heads of families (Acts 15. 2, 4, 6, 22, 23).[4] The decision is in no way represented as monarchic, and it is certainly an anachronism to speak of a hierarchy at this stage of development. The decision to select the Seven and the selection itself were made by the Twelve and "all the disciples" (Acts 6. 2).

It is not my intention to evade the pastoral epistles, nor to draw any arguments for anything from the critical agreement that the pastoral epistles are deutero-Pauline. They certainly describe aspects of the Church of the New Testament, not the post-apostolic or Ignatian Church, and they exhibit a better defined structure than the earlier New Testament writings. But the official titles used do not escape the ambiguity of the titles used in earlier books; the pastoral epistles still know no hierarchy and no monarchy. They do not clearly repudiate the democratic features suggested by the decisions reached in the book of Acts.

The New Testament Church drew nothing from either Jewish or pagan antecedents. The Greek word *hiereus*, priest, is not

[3] Dillon-Fitzmyer in *Jerome Biblical Commentary* (1968), 45:72.
[4] John L. McKenzie, "The Elders in the Old Testament", *Analecta Biblica*, 10 (1959), pp. 388–406.

used of church officers, although it is used of Jewish priests. No church officer corresponds to the scribes of Judaism, who were not really official but did exercise power. Nothing indicates that the "teachers" of the New Testament exercised a corresponding power. The sayings of Jesus in Matt. 23 scarcely recommend the scribe as a model of Christian authority. Essential to the influence of the scribe was the Torah of whose authority he was the interpreter. Both the gospels and Paul left no room for a Christian Torah. The development of the Christian law is much later than biblical times. So was the adoption of a pagan Roman religious title, *Romanus Pontifex*, for an office for which the New Testament has no word.

III. The Cultic Ministry

If we look at the cultic ministry, we find that there is no one in the New Testament to whom the cultic ministry is officially and exclusively committed, a striking omission in a Jewish-Hellenistic culture which knew much cultic officers in abundance. Indeed it is difficult to define the cult of the New Testament Church. Certainly cultic rites included baptism, the Eucharist and public common prayer. The Twelve, the apostles and the Seven baptized; we do not know who did not baptize. Paul himself put the proclamation of the Gospel above the ministry of baptism in his own mission (1 Cor. 1. 17). It cannot be established that the apostolic Church had already arrived at the practice, traditional for us, which permitted any human being to baptize, but we cannot establish the restrictions of the apostolic Church either. Paul insists that it makes no difference who confers baptism (1 Cor. 1. 11–16). We may speak of the ministry of baptism; we may not speak of a ministerial class which is empowered to baptize.

There is scarcely less ambiguity about the ministry of the Eucharist. Certainly this was the major and peculiarly Christian cultic act from the beginning of the Christian communities. In the four narratives of the institution, the Eleven (or the Twelve?) are instructed to repeat the consumption of bread and wine, declared to be the body and blood of Jesus, in his memory. The New Testament does not understand the precept of repetition as a precept to "consecrate", as the word consecrate has been long understood in Roman Catholic theology. It is understood as a precept to repeat the meal, and the power of "consecration" is not even understood as vested in the Church, much less in a ministerial class. The picture of the supper suggested in 1 Cor. 11. 17–22 suggests groups formed according to families or some other social connection. Who uttered the "words of consecration"? We cannot apply to these early assemblies the later eucharistic priesthood or anything like it. That the worshipping group had presiding officers must be assumed, for we know that each church had presiding officers, even if we do not know their titles or functions. But these officers were not set apart by a power of orders which enabled them to consecrate the Eucharist.

Even less are we assured that any officer was empowered or appointed to lead the community in prayer. We do not doubt that someone or several did lead in prayer; it is a question whether the leadership was a function of a ministry established precisely for that purpose. A father normally leads his family in prayer, but he does not lead in virtue of an ordained ministry. The model for most Christian assemblies of worship must have been the synagogue, and the synagogue had men who were appointed to read, to teach and to lead in prayer. Those who performed these offices were not priests and had no ritual consecration. If we must refer again to Corinth, it is to notice that leadership in prayer there was more clearly the fruit of charismatic impulse than of official appointment (1 Cor. 14. 14–17).

IV. The Ministry of Preaching and Teaching

The primacy which Paul gave to preaching in his own mission is in harmony with other parts of the New Testament, ranging from the commission which Matthew (28. 18–20) attributes to Jesus to the pastoral epistles, which are presumed to illustrate the most recent ecclesiastical developments of the New Testament period (1 Tim. 4. 13; 2 Tim. 4. 1–5). Paul attributes to the word a power which is not only charismatic, it approaches the sacramental (Rom. 1. 16–17). The commission of the apostle to preach the word is the clearest example of genuine ministerial office in the New Testament. Paul nearly always identifies himself as an apostle of Jesus Christ (Rom. 1. 1; 1 Cor. 1. 1; 2 Cor. 1. 1), and on occasion he is compelled to emphasize that he is not an apostle by human commission (Gal. 1. 1). Yet Paul's references to letters of accreditation (2 Cor. 3. 1–3) show that some evidence of human approval was expected. His references to the possibility of "another Gospel" which the Galatians should reject, even if an angel proclaimed it, show that the Gospel had a recognizable content (Gal. 1. 8–9). In the context of Paul's saying, the content is that only Jesus Christ saves, and that no one can contribute anything to his saving work.

Once all this is said, we have to recognize that many besides the apostles were engaged in the proclamation of the Gospel, and that we cannot suppose a constant supervision such as is exercised in the modern Church. The supervision suggested by the letters of Paul was certainly occasional rather than regular; indeed, one who insisted that he was accountable to no man must have had some difficulty in principle in discussing his Gospel with the "pillars" of the Jerusalem church (Gal. 2. 1–10). It seems that Paul did exactly "discuss" without conceding to anyone the right to examine him; he examined them as much as they examined him. The Seven were chosen in the Jerusalem church for "the ministry of tables" while the Twelve reserved themselves for "prayer and the ministry of the word" (Acts 6. 2–4). Yet some of the Seven appear as engaged in the ministry of the word (Acts 6. 10; 8. 5), and it is impossible to tell whether the inconsistency lies in Luke or in the practice of the primitive Church. If we have here an official ministry—and the Twelve and Seven seem to be so distinguished—then the distinction of ministerial functions is anything but sharp.

Somewhere in "the ministry of the word" we ought to find a place for prophets, evangelists and teachers (1 Cor. 12. 28; Eph. 4. 11). There is very little clear evidence what the prophet was in the New Testament Church. The texts indicate that he was a charismatic speaker, not an official; the texts do not indicate what he said. The evangelist can scarcely be distinguished from anyone else who under another title proclaims the Gospel. The teacher suggests the Jewish scribe; and indeed there are indications from the use of the words "teacher" and "teaching" that the teaching was the explanation of the Old Testament in a Christological sense. What is in no way suggested by the words is a ministry of authoritative teaching in the sense in which *magisterium*, the teaching office, has become one of the major ministerial functions in the Roman Catholic Church. In the New Testament teaching was directed to believers, and not certainly to all of them. The outward thrust of the Church, its "apostolic" character, was fulfilled in the ministry of proclamation. The question may be asked whether the outward thrust is incorporated in any official ministry of the contemporary Church.

V. The NT and Pluriform Ministerial Structures Today

This survey permits us to turn finally to the question which this paper is intended to treat: what is the significance of the ministerial structure of the New Testament for pluriform ministerial structures in the Church today? First of all, it is obvious that pluriform structure is general in the New Testament. Nothing suggests a uniform structure imposed from above. This does not imply that development beyond the New Testament is impossible or undesirable; it does imply that such a development, when it occurred, was based on other than biblical reasons. To the degree to which these reasons were historical other structures can be suggested by other historical reasons. Pluriformity is not contrary to the New Testament, whatever else it may be contrary to.

To be specific, the New Testament not only permits but is the source of the permanent diaconate; and the Roman Catholic Church has the problem of explaining why it ever allowed this New Testament institution to lapse. No explanation of its restoration is necessary. Celibate ministry is nowhere recommended in the New Testament, and no association of ministry and celibacy is even implied. Again, the problem of the Roman Catholic Church is to explain why celibacy was ever attached to the ministry. There is no more need to explain the marriage of clergy than there is to explain the marriage of laity. Two other questions may be raised.

The first question is whether ecumenical reunion demands that the entire ministry be structured in the Roman Catholic sense, or whether a truly ecumenical Church would have room for both Catholic and Protestant structures. The New Testament contains nothing which would impose uniformity; it even appears, although our lack of information makes a definitive statement impossible, that such pluriform ecumenical structures would not exceed in diversity the ministerial structures of the New Testament Church. Once again, at the risk of becoming tedious, it is necessary to point out that the Roman Catholic Church has the problem of explaining why it has adopted titles and offices which the New Testament does not use.

The second question is the ministry of women. The New Testament knew the "ministry" of women; quotation marks are necessary because the word has since acquired meanings which *diakonia* did not have (Rom. 16. 1). We can wish Paul had said more about the place of Priscilla in the structure (Acts 18. 26; Rom. 16. 3–5; 1 Cor. 16. 19), and how he would reconcile her position with his remarks in 1 Cor. 14. 33–36). Perhaps we see an inconsistency which Paul did not. We have rigorously universalized 1 Cor. 14. 33–36 far beyond its context; we have not been equally rigorous with Gal. 3. 28, a verse which admits the ministry of women as clearly as any biblical passage admits anything. On the other hand, Paul was a Jew; and it must be remembered that in Judaism women are not full religious persons.[5] I think Gal. 3. 28 attests that Paul rose above his Judaism, and that 1 Cor. 14. 33–36 attests that he did not always remain at the level to which he rose at least once. It is time for the Christian churches to ask whether their ministerial structures have echoed Paul's Judaism or Paul's Christianity.

[5] G. F. Moore, *Judaism* (1927), II, pp. 126–31. Moore's treatment is quaintly dated. After citing such things as the rabbinical *minyan* (ten adult males are necessary for synagogue worship) he remarks that the social and religious position of women in Judaism is a moral achievement. This moral achievement happened in a culture in which a celebrated rabbi said that a man ought to thank God daily that God did not make him a Gentile, a woman or ignorant (Strack-Billerbeck, *Kommentar zum NT aus Talmud und Midraschim* [1926] III, p. 611).

Harry McSorley

Recognition of a Presbyteral Succession?

A previous number of this journal contained several essays illustrating the growing awareness among Catholic theologians that the apostolicity of the Church and apostolic succession are not to be equated with or reduced to the historic succession of bishops within the Church as many Catholic and Anglo-Catholic theologians have previously thought.[1] The newer tendency, based on a fuller study of the testimony of the ancient Church, is to see apostolicity as an attribute of the whole Church, involving a succession to or continuation of the apostolic faith, life, mission, teaching, witness and service.

In this view of apostolicity the succession of bishops is by no means overlooked. One refuses, of course, to maximize the significance of the historic succession of bishops in such a way that Christian communities not possessing or laying claim to the historic episcopate are, by that very fact, not a part of the Christian Church. Such an understanding of the need for episcopacy has been excluded by the teaching of the Second Vatican Council that it is by faith and baptism that one is incorporated into the Body of Christ (cf. *Decree on Ecumenism*, n. 3).[2] On the other hand, the value of the historic succession of bishops is by no means minimized. Without suggesting that what follows

[1] *Concilium*, Vol. 4 (April 1968); U.S. edn., Vol. 34.
[2] Cf. K. McDonnell, "The Concept of 'Church' in the Documents of Vatican II..." in *Lutherans and Catholics in Dialogue IV: Eucharist and Ministry* [=*Luth/Cath*] (Washington, New York, 1970), pp. 307-24.

is an exhaustive statement on the meaning of the historic episcopate, it is important to underscore the growing agreement among Catholic and Prostestant theologians that, in addition to the widely recognized pastoral, prophetic and priestly functions of the bishop, the succession of bishops is a sign (efficacious when properly realized) "of the apostolic succession of the ministry and of the Church, and therefore a sign of the unity and catholicity of the Church."[3]

Leaving aside here the question of recognition of what has been called the succession of prophetic or charismatic ministries operative in the various Christian communities,[4] we wish to address ourselves to the question, how is the Roman Catholic Church to assess the ministries of those churches, such as the Lutheran and the Presbyterian, where the historic succession of bishops has not been maintained, but where an orderly succession of pastors or ministers has been continued through ordination by laying on of hands, the hands, however, not of a bishop, but of a priest/pastor? Some theologians argue that the very fact that non-episcopal bodies are churches or possess ecclesial reality—something that was recognized by the Second Vatican Council—implies the presence of true ministries in those churches. This line of reasoning has been called the "ecclesiological validation" of non-episcopal ministries.[5] When we look at the justification given by the Lutheran reformers for the authenticity of the "second generation" of their ministers, we find that they appeal not only to "ecclesiological validation" but also to "ritual validation", that is, to the legitimacy of ordinations conferred by the laying on of hands, even though the hands are those of a previously ordained pastor/priest and not a bishop.[6]

We shall first present the rationale for a presbyteral succession which we find in the official Lutheran confessional books, touching only briefly the similar passages in Calvin's *Institutes*. We

³ Cf. W. A. Quanbeck, "A Contemporary View of Apostolic Succession," in: *Luth/Cath*, 187 and "Reflections of the R. C. Participants," *ibid.*, pp. 32 f., n. 57.
⁴ Cf. A. Dulles, "The Succession of Prophets in the Church," *Concilium*, *loc. cit.* (n. 1), and K. McDonnell, "Ways of Validating Ministry," *Journ Ecum. Stud.* 7 (1970), pp. 244–54.
⁵ McDonnell, "Ways...", pp. 254–63.
⁶ *Ib.*, pp. 217–44.

will then offer an historical and theological critique of this argumentation, followed by some conclusions and implications for the contemporary ecumenical situation.

I. PRESBYTERAL ORDINATION/SUCCESSION IN REFORMATION DOCUMENTS

In the *Apology of the Augsburg Confession* (1531), made an official part of the Lutheran confessions of faith in 1537, we read: "...We have given testimony...to our deep desire to maintain the church polity and various ranks of the ecclesiastical hierarchy, although they were created by human authority. We know that the Fathers had good and useful reasons for instituting ecclesiastical discipline in the manner described by the ancient canons. But the bishops either force our priests to forsake and condemn the sort of doctrine we have confessed, or else... they kill the unfortunate and innocent men.... Thus the cruelty of the bishops is the reason for the abolition of canonical government in some places, despite our earnest desire to keep it."[7]

What this text shows is that, despite their desire to remain in union with the bishops of the Roman Church, even to the point of having ministers ordained according to the "form of law and ecclesiastical ordinances and decrees hitherto observed everywhere in the Christian world", as the papal theologians had demanded,[8] the early Lutherans believed pastoral necessity justified their setting aside the ecclesiastical regulations concerning ordination.

"The Church must not be deprived of ministers" because of the negative stance of the Catholic bishops, says Luther in the the *Smalcald Articles* of 1537. "Accordingly," he continues, "as we are taught by the examples of the ancient churches and Fathers, we shall and ought ourselves ordain suitable persons to this office. The papists have no right to forbid or prevent us, not even according to their own laws, for their laws state that those who are ordained by heretics shall also be regarded as ordained.

[7] Art. 14, *The Book of Concord*, tr. T. G. Tappert (Philadelphia, 1959) [=Tappert] 214 f. (*Die Bekenntnisschriften d. evang.-luth. Kirche*, Göttingen,[6] 1967).

[8] *Confutatio, Corpus Reformatorum* 27 (Berlin, 1859), pp. 114 f.

... St Jerome, too, wrote concerning the church in Alexandria that it was originally governed without bishops by priests and preachers in common."[9]

It is not clear to which laws Luther is referring. The references to Gratian's *Decretum* given by the editors of the critical edition of the Lutheran confessions are likewise unhelpful. It is true that, after much vacillation, the validity of baptism and ordination conferred by heretics and schismatics came to be recognized by the medieval Church. The underlying assumption, however, was that the one ordaining was himself a validly consecrated *bishop*, whereas the new Lutheran pastors were being ordained by priests.

The argument which invokes St Jerome is much more formidable than the canonical argument. In the *Smalcald Articles* it is more an allusion than an argument. For the full development of the argument we must look at Melanchthon's *Treatise on the Power and Primacy of the Pope*,[10] also written in 1537. There Jerome's *Letter 146 to Evangelus* is cited—according to the version of it found in Gratian's *Decretum*[11]—in which Jerome states that in the early Church, the *episcopus* and the *presbyter* were the same. For the sake of avoiding schism, however, observes Jerome, "one man was chosen over the rest ... lest several persons, by gathering separate followings around themselves, rend the Church of Christ. For in Alexandria, from the time of Mark the Evangelist to the time of Bishops Heracles [sic] and Dionysius, the presbyters always chose one of their number, set him in a higher place, and called him bishop.... For, apart from ordination, what does a bishop do that a presbyter does not do?"

Thus far the citation from Jerome. Now for Melanchthon's argument based on it: "Jerome ... teaches that the distinction between the grades of bishop and presbyter (or pastor) is by human authority.... Afterwards one thing made a distinction between bishops and pastors, and this was ordination, for it was decided that one bishop should ordain the ministers in a number

[9] *Smal. Art.*, III, 10; Tappert, p. 314.

[10] Nn. 60–7; Tappert, pp. 330 f.

[11] P. I, D. 93, c. 24, *Corp. Iur. Can.: Decretum*, ed. A. Friedberg (Leipzig, 1879), pp. 327–9.

of churches. But since the distinction between bishop and pastor is not by divine right, it is manifest that ordination administered by a pastor in his own church is valid by divine right. Consequently, when the regular bishops become enemies of the Gospel and are unwilling to administer ordination, the churches retain the right to ordain for themselves. For wherever the Church exists, the right to administer the Gospel also exists. Wherefore it is necessary for the Church to retain the right of calling, electing, and ordaining ministers."[12]

Melanchthon correctly states Jerome's doctrine on the presbyter-bishop relationship even though he does not adduce Jerome's *Commentary on Titus* in which it is explicitly stated that the bishops know they are superior (*majores*) to priests more by custom than by a disposition of the Lord.[13]

In his *Institutes*, Calvin uses both Jerome texts, even though he does not argue the case for presbyteral succession as rigorously as Melanchthon. Neither for Calvin nor for Melanchthon does the *idea* of succession play an important role in the doctrine of ordination. Both agree, however, that ordination is by solemn imposition of hands by those already ordained.[14]

II. EVALUATION OF THE CASE FOR PRESBYTERAL SUCCESSION

The final two sentences of Melanchthon's argument for the authenticity of presbyteral ordination are a succinct statement of what has been referred to above as an ecclesiological validation of a non-episcopal ministry. A number of Catholic theologians would find in this argument alone sufficient reason for the recognition of the ministries of at least some non-episcopal churches.

In assessing the effort of the Lutherans to defend the authenticity of their newly ordained pastors we also find a claim for a ritual validation in which the testimony of St Jerome is crucial. This testimony involves (1) the *biblical-theological* position that there was no original difference between *presbyteri* and *episcopi*

[12] *Treatise*, nn. 64–7.
[13] P.L. 26, 598.
[14] Cf. *Institutes* IV, 4, 2 and J. Burleigh, "The Presbyter in Presbyterianism," *Scot. Jl. of Theol.* 2 (1949), p. 304.

and that the later differentiation which gave the *episcopi* the ascendancy—including the function of ordaining—was due to church custom, not the command of the Lord; and (2) the *historical* claim that, until the third century in Alexandria, it was a college of presbyters and not a bishop that elected from their own ranks the new bishop on the death of his predecessor.

Concerning the historical question, Charles Gore and Cuthbert Turner and, more recently, Joseph Lécuyer, are among those who have found serious historical reasons to question the reliability of the testimony of Jerome, more or less corroborated by Severus and Antioch and the tenth-century Eutychius of Alexandria, concerning the church at Alexandria.[15] They argue that what Jerome reported as historical fact was actually a twisted version of a slanderous rumour circulated by the Arians against Athanasius, namely, that he was not a true bishop because he had only been ordained by presbyters. Eric W. Kemp thinks this argument has some plausibility, but believes it rests on an argument from silence that is "too ambiguous to be built upon."[16]

In the course of his essay, Kemp severely criticizes some of the argumentation and conclusions of W. Telfer, who also dealt with this historical situation at Alexandria.[17] It would be a mistake, however, to see Kemp's critique as a total rejection of Telfer's conclusions.[18] The main thrust of Kemp's criticism was directed at Telfer's intemperate polemic against Gore, especially in regard to Telfer's loose equation of "the principle of apostolic succession with the idea of consecration by a series of monarchical bishops"[19]—a mistake still prevalent among Catholics as was suggested at the beginning of this article. Kemp's own con-

---

[15] Gore, *The Church and the Ministry*, new ed. revised by C. H. Turner (London, 1936), p. 115; Lécuyer, "Le problème des consécrations épiscopales dans l'Eglise d'Alexandrie," *Bull. de Litt. Eccl.* 65 (1964), pp. 241-57.

[16] "Bishops and Presbyters at Alexandria," *Journ. of Eccl. Hist.* 6 (1955), p. 137.

[17] "Episcopal Succession in Egypt," *Journ. of Eccl. Hist.* 3 (1952), pp. 1-13.

[18] Cf. E. Kilmartin, "The Eucharist in Recent Literature," *Theol. Studies* 32 (1971), p. 272; and J. Lécuyer, *Bull. de Litt. Eccl.* 70 (1969), pp. 81-99.

[19] Kemp, p. 142.

clusion as to the historical situation at Alexandria is that there "is evidence that there was a carefully regulated succession, albeit a succession through a presbyteral college." Despite many obscurities, he continues, the Alexandrian case emphasizes "that the principle of apostolic succession is compatible with a presbyterian constitution."[20]

Whatever one's judgment as to the shape of the ministry in early Alexandria, it is interesting to note that the indisputable historical evidence showing that priest/presbyters have the radical capacity to ordain other presbyters was apparently unknown to the reformers: the well-attested cases of presbyteral ordinations conferred by presbyters in the fifteenth century.[21] Ludwig Ott questions the alleged presbyteral ordinations by Willihad and Liudger in the eighth century, but has no doubts that in the fifteenth century priests acted as extraordinary ministers of the sacrament of the presbyteral order.[22]

As W. Kasper has rightly noted, "We find in the Middle Ages not only the practice of, but also the theoretical reflection on a presbyteral succession."[23] What we noted above should also be recalled: Jerome is witness not simply to an alleged fact about the Alexandrian church order, but also to a biblical-theological theory according to which differences between presbyter and bishop are of ecclesiastical, not divine, institution. Similar views were held by John Chrysostom, Ambrosiaster and Pelagius.[24] This current of thought remained alive not only among the later canonists, but also among the early scholastic exegetes and theologians as well as in Gratian's *Decretum*, where we read: "A priest is the same as a bishop and it is only by custom that bishops preside over priests."[25]

Is it any wonder, in the face of this strong doctrinal, canonical and historical tradition, that the Council of Trent refused to

[20] *Ibid.*, p. 143.
[21] Cf. A. C. Piepkorn in *Luth/Cath*, 220–6; W. Kasper, "Zur Frage der Anerkennung der Ämter in den lutherischen Kirchen," *Theol. Quartal.* 151 (1971), pp. 99–104.
[22] Cf. *Hand. d. Dogmengesch.*, IV/5, Freiburg, 1969, p. 59, n. 1 and pp. 106 f.
[23] *Op. cit.*, p. 101.
[24] Kemp, pp. 125–8.
[25] P. I, D. 95, c. 5; Friedberg, p. 332; cf. Ott, p. 46.

accept the proposal that the difference between presbyter and bishop was of divine institution?[26] Such a definition would not only have condemned the continental reformers, but a great number of Catholic theologians and canonists as well, including at least two Fathers of the Church. When we look at the Tridentine state of the question in this way it is also easier for us to understand why the council's only criticism of pastors who had not been ordained by "canonical and ecclesiastical power" was that they were not "legitimate" ministers of word and sacrament. Such ministries are not declared to be "null and void" or "invalid" but simply not "legitimate" inasmuch as they violated the long-standing discipline of the Church.[27] Nor do we find at Trent any criticism or rejection of Melanchthon's arguments for the authenticity of ministers who had, out of necessity, been extraordinarily ordained by other priests.

Even after the Second Vatican Council a Catholic theologian is free to hold that, under certain circumstances, an ordinary priest may ordain another priest. As we read in the official *relatio* to n. 21 of the *Constitution on the Church*: "The Commission decided that nothing should be declared concerning the question, whether only a bishop can ordain priests and therefore it has settled neither the question of law nor of fact."[28]

It has been suggested that the presbyteral theory operative within Catholicism at least since the time of Jerome, and which came to life in the Middle Ages when papal permission was given certain abbots to ordain men to the priesthood, is not really an argument "for presbyterianism but for popery."[29] What is being criticized here, of course, is the view that it is only with and because of papal authorization that a priest can validly ordain another priest. While many Catholic theologians would undoubtedly subscribe to such a view, it seems to me to be an equally legitimate Catholic opinion, in light of what has already

---

[26] Cf. G. Fahrnberger, *Bischofsamt und Priestertum in den Diskussionen des Konzils v. Trient* (Vienna, 1970).

[27] Cf. *Denz.-Schön.* 1777 and my essay "Trent and the Question: Can Protestant Ministers Consecrate the Eucharist?" in *Luth/Cath.*, pp. 283–99. I find it odd that Kilmartin, *op. cit.*, p. 269, thinks it is *my* "view that Trent saw the ministries of Reformation churches as 'illegitimate'."

[28] *Schema Constitutionis de Ecclesia* (Vatican, 1964), p. 87.

[29] E. L. Mascall, *The Recovery of Unity* (London, [2]1959), p. 213.

been said, to hold that, while it would not be legitimate or licit, according to the medieval and present-day discipline of the Church, for a priest so to act without papal authorization when there is no moral necessity to do so, one might well conceive of extraordinary situations, such as a time of persecution, where it would be both valid and legitimate for a priest to ordain other men to the priesthood if no bishop were available. Following the lead of contemporary Catholic Luther scholarship in predicating good faith of the early reformers and granting that it was a genuine religious motivation that led them to try to reform the Church—however one might criticize their tactics or their doctrine—it would likewise seem that, on the basis of the theology of ministry and of the Eucharist found in the Lutheran symbolic books, one could also conclude to the presence of an authentic ministry via the presbyteral succession. What this means in short is that the need to have papal permission or authorization before a priest exercises the role of extraordinary minister of the sacrament of order is a requirement of ecclesiastical law which can be set aside for serious reason.

In view of the clear command of Christ that Christians are to live in unity, the burden of proof lies with those who think such papal permission is required by a divine, immutable law that cannot be set aside under any circumstances whatever.

III. Conclusions and Ecumenical Implications

1. The argument used by the early Lutherans to defend the authenticity of presbyteral ordination is one that is at least highly probable. It is one of the several reasons that prompted fourteen Roman Catholic theologians, including two bishops, to state: "We have found serious defects in the arguments customarily used against the validity of the eucharistic Ministry of the Lutheran churches. In fact, we see no persuasive reason to deny the possibility of the Roman Catholic Church recognizing the validity of this Ministry."[30]

2. The argument is an argument on behalf of what is today commonly called the validity of such ordinations. This means

[30] *Luth/Cath*, 23, n. 40 and 32, n. 54.

that recognition of this presbyteral succession by the Roman Catholic Church would not involve the bestowal of an intrinsic validity on those properly ordained in the presbyteral succession, but simply an official acknowledgment of this validity by the Roman Catholic Church. This would render unnecessary any reconciliation service that would involve either unilateral or mutual laying on of hands, the ambiguity of which has already proven to be a stumbling-block in other efforts to reunite episcopal and non-episcopal churches.

3. Given the willingness of the official Lutheran confessions to recover the historic episcopal polity of the Church, given the increasing readiness of contemporary Lutheran theologians to see the episcopal succession not simply as a long-standing form of church organization but as an eminent sign of the apostolic succession of the whole Church, and given the obligation of all Christians to work for the fulfilment of the clear expression of Christ's will that his followers live in the closest possible unity, the only thing that would prevent the Roman Catholic Church from recognizing the Lutheran ministry would be evidence that there is an equally clear expression of Christ's will that such recognition is impossible. To my knowledge, no one has yet offered such evidence.

Ordination—A Sacrament?

1. *An Orthodox Reply*

John Zizioulas

I. THE THEOLOGICAL PERSPECTIVE

IN order to answer the question concerning the sacramental character of ordination from the point of view of Orthodox theology, it is in the first place necessary to set the theological perspective in which Eastern Orthodox theology would place ordination. The subject of "sacrament" and of ordination as a "sacrament" was practically raised in the West on the basis of a sacramental theology to which the East was fundamentally a stranger. It is, of course, true that the East did enter the discussion which took place in the sixteenth and seventeenth centuries between Roman Catholic and Protestant theologians in an attempt to establish the "Orthodox position" in the spirit of confessionalism which prevailed at that time.[1] The task, however, was by no means an easy one, and what these documents managed to do was simply to take arguments from the Protestant side and use them against the Roman Catholic positions, and *vice versa*, thus establishing a *via media* between the two, whenever possible. This exercise proved not only unsuccessful but in a way unfortunate, since it deprived the East of the possibility of offering its own distinctive contribution—a contribution which would affect the theological perspective itself. This point can be more clearly seen and appreciated in our time when the revival of biblical, patristic and liturgical studies, and above all the decisive overcoming, in many ways, of Scholasticism by Vatican II, have shown how important a change of perspective may be for ecumenical dialogue.

[1] Cf., e.g., the "Confessions" of Peter Mogila, Dositheus, etc.

The main components of the theological perspective in which Eastern theology, as it developed mainly at the time of the Greek Fathers, would see this question, could be summarized as follows:

(a) It is impossible to treat the sacraments and ordination as *autonomous* subjects. Both of them form *aspects* of the one indivisible mystery which is indicated by *Christology*.

(b) Christology itself cannot be treated as an autonomous subject: it is to be conditioned constantly by *Pneumatology*, and as such it is to be organically related to *Ecclesiology*. This brings Trinitarian Theology itself into Ecclesiology.

(c) Ecclesiology in its being related to Christology in and through Pneumatology is to be conceived in terms of (i) Eschatology, as an inevitable component of Pneumatology (cf. Acts 2), and (ii) the concrete *community* of the local church as a natural creation of the *communion* of the Holy Spirit.

(d) There is a broader *cosmic* dimension to be recognized in this approach: what happens in the sacraments and in ordination concerns the entire creation and not simply man.

This perspective suggests that we look at the question of the sacramental character of ordination from the angle of the concrete community of the Church before we come to consider it from the point of view of the ordained person himself.

II. THE "ORDAINED" AND THE COMMUNITY

There are certain liturgical and practical elements in ordination which theologians tend to bypass in constructing their views on the ministry, but which for the liturgically-minded tradition of the East form the very starting-point of theological inquiry. I have in mind particularly the following two principles going back to the earliest tradition of the Church, both in the West and in the East: (a) no ordination can take place outside the eucharistic assembly of the local church; and (b) no ordination can be "absolute", i.e. without binding the ordained person to a concrete community.

The first theological implication of this tradition is that ordination is not to be understood in terms of an objectified and transmitted grace or *potestas*, but as an act by which the Holy Spirit establishes particular relationships within the community of the Church. This idea of "relationship" should not be understood in the sense of an abstract and logical *relatio*, but as having a deeply existential and soteriological meaning. In Greek patristic tradition this would include two aspects: (a) a relational reality which unites the community itself in dividing it into ministries (the Church through ordination is "united in division"—*sundiairoumenē*: St Maximus the Confessor); and (b) an act by which the Church, and through it mankind and creation, are brought into a reconciling relation with God (ministry as "ambassadorship"—*presbeia*: St John Chrysostom). In this sense, ordination does nothing but realize the ministry of Christ here and now and within a concrete existential situation, by establishing a ministry not *parallel* to but *identical* with that of Christ, so that in fact Christ will remain the only Minister in the Church (Chrysostom).[2]

Another fundamental implication is that ordination cannot be understood in terms of *causality*. The notion of causality is responsible for many problems concerning ordination which are still being discussed. Hence the question whether ordination brings upon the ordained grace and authority through the channel of a *jure divino* instituted medium (e.g., the bishop in the line of apostolic succession) arises from a notion of sacramental causality. Opponents of apostolic succession still work with the idea of causality by making the community itself the source or the medium of the authority given by ordination. In the ancient Eastern tradition, however, ordination does not pass through any process of causality, but represents a divine act realized *as part of the eucharistic community*. The bishop must be understood as ordaining precisely *as the head of this community*, and not as an individual. Had he been acting as an individual, he could perform ordinations in his study. The writings attributed to Dionysius the Areopagite in an extreme denial of sacramental causality state that in ordination the bishop ordains "not by his own movement (gesture) but by the divine movement...". This has nothing to do with the monophysitic tendencies usually attributed to these writings; it is simply the typical *epicletic*

---

[2] This goes back to the New Testament in which *all* ministerial titles known to the primitive Church are attributed to Christ.

approach of the East. The liturgical formula of ordination itself reveals the same approach in (a) making God the subject of the verb "ordain" ("The divine grace...ordains"), and (b) requiring that the community sing the *kyrie eleison* during the moment of ordination. The meaning of all this is that ordination depends essentially *on prayer* and not on an objective sacramental causality as such. Apostolic succession is not absent in this way of thinking but it is understood in terms of a charismatic *identity of the communities* (through their heads) in time and space.

In attaching to the community such importance we must not imply that the community *precedes* the individual ordination in a sense, again, of causality. We cannot speak of a *charismatic nature* of the community representing, so to say, the source and the generic principle of the particular ministries. This charismatic essentialism would seem to imply that we have *first* a charismatic nature (= community) and *then* particular charismata (= ordinations). If, for example, the idea of the "priesthood of all believers" is to be understood in this way, it immediately becomes alien to Eastern theology. What then can we say about the particular charismata in relation to the community?

The answer to this question lies in the fact that the particular charismata do not *follow* the existence of the Body of Christ, but are *constitutive* of it. Here the mystery of the Church—and of Christology—becomes absolutely dependent on pneumatology: the Body of Christ is constituted and defined by the concrete charismata.[3] The conclusion is that ordination is *a primordial and constitutive act of the Christian community.*

This primordial character of ordination is to be seen in the fact that there is actually no such a person as a "non-ordained" member of the Church. It is a mistake to call the lay members of the Church "non-ordained". Baptism and especially confirmation (chrismation) as an inseparable aspect of the rite of initiation involves a "laying on of hands" and a "seal" (*sphragis*), and *inevitably and immediately* leads the baptized person to the eucharistic community in order to assume his particular *"ordo"* there. The laity do not represent either a morally lower or a generically general and "prior" kind of charismatic existence, but exist *together with* the other orders.

[3] This also follows from an attentive study of 1 Cor. 12.

In this way of thinking the question whether the "ordained" person differs from the layman *"essentia"* or simply *"gradu"* becomes irrelevant. We should rather approach the difference between the two in terms of a *specificity of relationship* within the Church. When in the ancient Eastern Church the word "grade" is used for ordination (e.g., in the Areopagetic writings) it is not understood as a *stage* in the progress or development of a certain sacramental essence, but as *part of the entire mystery* which in Christ unites and reconciles creation to God. Each ordination, therefore, *constitutes anew* the Church in a pneumatological way.[4] The Church through ordination comes into being here and now as the Body of Christ. Its "becoming" is not *derived* from its being—there is no law of causality operating in this approach.

III. Implications for the "Ordained" Person

In describing the difference between an "ordained" person and a "layman" in terms of "specificity of relationship" within the community, we risk being understood as implying something merely *functional*. Classical theology, under the influence of a certain ontologism with which Western philosophy has worked for centuries, has made us think in terms of the dilemma: ontological versus functional, leaving us with no possibility for a third choice.[5] This, however, cannot fit into our perspective here. An "ontology" which can be conceived or spoken of in itself without its *relational* character is incompatible with pneumatology, which makes everything dependent on *communion*. Equally, a "function" which has no ontological content denotes something utilitarian which may be conceivable in a purely human society, but is sheer blasphemy when applied to the communion of the Holy Spirit. What is affected of man in ordination is to be understood neither in "ontological" nor "functional", but in *personal* terms. "Personhood" as distinct both from "individuality" which objectifies and experiences man, and "per-

---

[4] In each episcopal ordination in the Orthodox Church the feast of Pentecost is celebrated.

[5] Orthodox theologians, too, have always felt obliged to work with this dilemma.

sonality" which psychologizes and evaluates man, is precisely a *relational* category which conditions being existentially.

The terms used by the Greek Fathers to indicate the specificity of the ordained priest are marked by this approach. Not only the notion of priesthood as "ambassadorship", to which we referred earlier, but even terms which appear to be "ontologistic" (e.g., "transfiguration"—St Gregory of Nyssa; "transmutation—*metastoicheiosis*"—St Cyril of Alexandria) are understood always in the sense of *participation*: the priest receives the grace "for those who need it" (Theodore Mops.) and as "part of" the eucharistic community (Gregory Nys.). It is a change described in terms of "honour", "glory", "dignity", etc. (Cyril Alex.), i.e., in terms of an anthropology of "theosis" which implies no ontological change, although it *affects* man in his being. As St Maximus the Confessor saw it, ordination is part of the Christological double movement between the Creator and creation— a movement which affects being, yet never statically but always as a *movement* and in the framework of a "cosmic liturgy".

In this understanding of the specificity of ordination there is, as in all pneumatologically conditioned ontology, an *eschatological character*. A term used for ordination in Greek patristic literature is that of "perfection" (*teleiosis*). This has again nothing to do with an "ontological" or "moral" perfection as such. It is to be understood rather with the help of two other terms used in the same literature, that of "type" (*typos*) or "place" (*topos*) (Ignatius Ant.; Const. Apost.), and "term" or "end" (*peras*) (Maximus Conf.). The ordained person is distinguished from the rest in that he is "like" (*hōsper*) or "in the place of" (*eis topon*) a particular person in the very kingdom of God. In the understanding of St Maximus this typology becomes dynamic: in and because of ordination (baptism being included) creation moves to its eschatological end: the eucharistic altar expresses here and now the potential eschatological nature of the community and —through it—of creation.

Ordination affects the ordained person in an eschatological sense. This is not to be understood in terms of an ontological *permanence* but of eschatological *decisiveness* and *finality*. The "specificity of relationship" realized in ordination is not just a temporal affair. The East, except perhaps in Nestorian circles, never distinguished strongly between the heavenly worship and the "cultum *praesentis* ecclesiae" (St Thomas Aquinas). In anthropological terms this means that no ordained person—whether "layman" or "clergyman"—can appear before God *pretending* that he has never been ordained. In this sense, ordination acts as a "seal" (*sphragis*)[6] on the ordained. This decisiveness in the character of ordination has nothing to do with ontology as such. Yet in its existential or personal nature it is very deep. If love will survive as the eschatological quintessence of the charismata (1 Cor. 13), ordination will emerge even more clearly and decisively, precisely because of its relational character.

IV. CONCLUDING REMARKS

It must have become clear from the above that the question put to us here cannot be answered in a direct way. In the perspective of ancient Eastern theology neither ordination nor sacrament can be objectified. In the notion of communion which becomes decisive in any pneumatologically understood ecclesiology there is a dynamic *ek-stasis* which makes the Church inconceivable as a being in itself vis-à-vis God. In this context the East has preferred the term "mystery" instead of "sacrament". Ordination reveals in a way the "eternal mystery" of God for creation, by distributing Christ's ministry in the unity of the Church, the *sacramentum mundi*. In this context any understanding of the ordained man in his ontology as such (*character indelibilis*, etc.) *defeats the very purpose of ordination*. Ordination creates an *ek-stasis* for the being, yet without "leaving behind" being in a mystical or functional[7] state. Ordination implies a transformation of the individual into a *person*, and in so doing it becomes decisive for him. The "grace" of sacramentalism is a "possessed" and "transmitted" object. In this sense ordination is not a sacrament. The grace of the mystery of Christ, i.e., the very love of God, is relational, and

---

[6] Widely used in the early Church both for baptism and ordination and implying among other things *ownership*: the sign by which God will recognize his own.

[7] Hence the notion of *service* (*diakonia*) used widely today for the ministry, although certainly defining it in a way, can at the same time be very misleading.

this means existentially decisive. In this sense, ordination can be called a "mystery".

2. *A Protestant Reply*

Jean-Jacques von Allmen

I. A QUESTION OF DEFINITION

I HAVE been asked to answer this question as a "Protestant", but since on this point, more perhaps than on any other, Protestantism is far from having a unanimous teaching, I shall answer as a member of the Eglise Reformée, relying on documents rather than on theology in the strict sense.

I begin with two quotations. The first is a text from Calvin: "With regard to the laying on of hands, which is performed to introduce true priests and ministers of the Church into their state, I have no objection at all to its being occepted as a sacrament. It is a ceremony taken from Scripture ... which is by no means empty ... but a sign of God's spiritual grace. If I have not placed it with the other two" (baptism and the Lord's Supper) "it is because it is not ordinary or common among the faithful, but for a particular office."[1] The other text is taken from the *Second Helvetic Confession* (1566): "The sacraments of the new people are baptism and the Lord's Supper. Some count seven sacraments under the New Testament; among which we recognize as things ordained by God and not as sacraments: penance, the institution of ministers ... and marriage."[2]

In the light of these texts, deciding whether or not ordination is one of the sacraments depends ultimately on the definition one gives of a sacrament. In the Reformed tradition only the signs instituted by Christ for the whole of the faithful and destined for them all are sacraments. Listing the sacraments in his *Cate-*

---

[1] *Institutes*, IV, 19, 28. See also IV, 19, 31.
[2] From the French version of 1566 (Neuchâtel, 1944), p. 112.

chism, Calvin said, "There are only two common sacraments, which the Lord Jesus instituted for the whole company of the faithful." If ordination is not counted among the sacraments, it is not because of a denial that it is one of the "things ordained by God", but because it is not common to all the faithful. The debate between "Catholic" and "Reformed" Christians on this point has nothing to do with the respect in which the ministry is or is not held; on both sides it is recognized as an institution of the Lord's which is constitutive of the Church. The debate centres on the definition of a sacrament, a definition which will enable us to say how many "ceremonies taken from Scripture" will be given the name "sacrament". Hence, if we say that ordination is not a sacrament, that does not mean that we think it has no connection with what Christ instituted for the creation and continuation of his Church; it means that it lacks one condition for being a sacrament; it is not conferred on all the faithful.[3]

II. The Four Elements of Ordination

It can be easily shown that the Reformed Church none the less takes ordination seriously by summarizing the four elements of its theological content.

1. Ordination is an *epiclesis* over a man to ask God to fill him with the charisms which will be necessary for the exercise of the ministry to which he is ordained. In the Zürich *Prädikantenordnung* (1552) the ordaining minister calls down the Spirit on the ordinand in these words: "May God give you his Holy Spirit, that you may act as a servant faithful to his master, in the name of God."[4] And in the liturgy approved at the nineteenth National

---

[3] It is true that this doctrine has often been eroded by the polemic conducted against it, and many members of my Church have doubted the importance of ordination *"because it is not a sacrament"*. Not being a sacrament would mean its being treated less seriously, rather as, for many Protestants, marriage loses its indissoluble character through not being a sacrament. There is a whole area of "sacramental psychology" here which it would be useful for the churches who recognize seven sacraments and those who recognize only two to study together. Many misunderstandings could be removed by such a dialogue.

[4] The quotations in this article are taken from my book, *Le saint ministère selon la conviction et la volonté des reformés du XVIe siècle* (Neuchâtel, 1968), pp. 47 ff.

Synod of the French Reformed churches (1609), we find the following prayer: "May it please thee, O God, to adorn with the gifts and graces of thy Holy Spirit this thy servant, legitimately elected according to the order established in thy Church, strengthening him abundantly with all the gifts necessary for the proper exercise of his charge, for the glory of thy holy name, for the building up of thy Church, and for the salvation of him who is now dedicated and consecrated to thee by our ministry...."

2. Ordination is also a dedication, and for this reason many Reformed churches, particularly French-speaking ones, are happier to talk of *consecration* than ordination; the laying on of hands is understood as a gesture of consecration: "this use is good and edifying, and according to the custom of the Apostles and to the practice of the ancient Church";[5] it is also deeply significant of what is taking place: "... the Apostles, by the laying on of hands, signified that they were offering to God him whom they were introducing to the ministry ... and indeed it is a useful thing to magnify the dignity of the ministry before the eyes of the people by such a ceremony, and also by the same to remind him who is ordained that he is no longer his own but is dedicated to the service of God and the Church."[6]

3. In its third aspect, ordination is an *authorization*: it allows the one ordained to preach the Gospel, to administer the sacraments and to be a shepherd to the people of God. When the ordination has taken place the faithful know that they are dealing with a genuine representative of the Lord, that they can trust him when he claims to act in the name of the Father, Son and Holy Spirit, that they will not be led astray if they follow him; and the minister himself knows that he is not a usurper when he administers the mysteries of God: he has the promise that God ratifies in heaven what he does on earth (with the proviso, of course, that what he does obeys the orders Christ gave to his apostles). Ordination also states what it gives authority to do: to proclaim the Word of God, to baptize and preside at the Eucharist, to lead the Church. The ministry for which ordination gives authority and power is thus one which takes up and continues the ministry entrusted to the apostles. If the ministers

[5] Fifth National Synod, Paris, 1565.
[6] Calvin, *Institutes*, IV, 3, 6.

entrusted with this apostolic function divide their responsibilities among themselves for the sake of good order, this division, and the diversified functions to which it gives rise, does not affect the nature of the ministry, nor therefore the *esse* of the Church. The Reformed Church has always considered that the differences between bishops and presbyters was merely sociological. This is the source of its conviction that ministers charged with the essential apostolic ministry of the proclamation of the Gospel, the administration of the sacraments and the leadership of the people of God, whether they are called "bishop" or "presbyter", are all equally capable of transmitting this ministry to others and are authorized to do so. On the other hand, if the ordinary ministers of the Church—whether they are called bishops, presbyters, pastors or doctors—need helpers to assist them in their tasks— men called "elders" or "deacons"—the helpers, with very rare exceptions, are not ordained, but simply installed in their ministry. This ministry is also often limited in time, whereas those who are ordained to the episcopal, pastoral or presbyteral ministry (the assumption is that, theologically speaking, these are all the same ministry) "should know that they have been chosen to be ministers all their lives".[7]

4. Finally, ordination places the one who is ordained in the line of successors of the apostles. It is a form of *spiritual generation* by which the ministry instituted by Christ perpetuates itself in the Church. If there are pastors in the Church, it is in obedience to the orders given "by Jesus Christ for the continual and ordinary government and perpetual preservation of his Church and the ministry of the same as long as it shall be in this world", in the words of P. Viret, one of Calvin's closest collaborators. I do not think it would be contradicting the deepest intention of the Reformers to say that in reforming the Church they wanted to recover the true apostolic succession, which in their eyes did not mean simply a legal pedigree but rather the faithful exercise of the ministry entrusted by Christ to the apostles. If this fourth characteristic of ordination is perhaps less strongly marked in the classical documents of the Reformation than the three others, it is none the less present, if only in the fact those

[7] Article 12 of the *Discipline* of the Reformed Churches of France, 1559.

who are charged with ordination to the pastoral ministry are themselves bearers of that ministry. This is to invoke the principle: *nemo possit dare quod non habet.*[8]

III. THE PERSONAL COMMITMENT OF THE CONSECRATED MINISTER

The demand made of the one consecrated to the ministry also shows how seriously ordination is taken in the Reformed Church: he is expected to give his consent to what is happening to him at his ordination, and to give his consent in perpetuity. Explaining the scope of this would involve me in a description of pastoral spirituality. I shall do no more than take up the four points just listed.

The minister has been exposed to the outpouring of the Spirit in order to receive from him the gifts necessary for the performance of his task: he must therefore "rekindle the gift of God" (cf. 2 Tim. 1. 6), and show by the way in which he gives himself to his task that he is not relying on his own strength alone to accomplish it. To be adequate to his task he can only ask that his ministry may become and be the answer to the prayers which the Church regularly addresses to God for the ministers, and thus also for him.

The minister's life is dedicated to the service of Christ in the Church. Unless he is to commit a sort of spiritual embezzlement and deprive God of what belongs to him, the minister has no right to use his life for anything other than the service of God. It is in this spiritual rather than legal perspective that we in our church prefer to approach the question of the indelible character of ordination; having agreed to be dedicated to the service of God, the minister is bound to his ministry. That is why the Reformation protested with relentless energy against clerical parasitism: having been offered to God in an ordination which was not forced upon him, but to which he gave his consent, the minister has committed himself to bringing about in practice the consecration of his life to the one to whom it has been conse-

---

[8] Maresius, *Collegium theologicum,* 1662, quoted by H. Heppe, *Die Dogmatik der reformierten Kirche* (Neukirchen, 1935), p. 547. See also my book mentioned in note 4, in particular the excursus, "la succession apostolique en ecclésiologie reformée", pp. 192–212.

crated. This is also the reason why it was not until the present day that the Protestant mind really felt the "professional" character of pastoral work as a problem, since it seemed so natural that a man whose whole life was dedicated to the service of the Gospel should indeed spend his life in that service and live by it.

We find the same thing, with a slightly different emphasis, if we look again at the third aspect of ordination: the authorization and legitimation which was then given to the minister was not given to him as a privilege which would make him a superior being; it was given to him to use, so that by using it he might be at the service of the salvation of those whom God had entrusted to him. In the sixteenth century we find a strong protest against those who do not carry out the task they are authorized to carry out, notably against an episcopate which took advantage of its dignity while the people died of hunger and thirst for spiritual food. If, albeit with a certain reticence, we use the term "clergy", it is not to designate a caste but to describe those who, on the basis of the authorization which has marked them off from the people, simply do what they have received authority to do.

Finally, the minister, through his ordination, knows that he has been made a part of the college of those who lead the people of God, part of the very process of the tradition of the Church. On the one hand he becomes the "colleague" of the other ministers—the determining role of this collegiality appears above all in the synodal structure of the Church—and on the other hand he is aware of a co-responsibility for tradition, charged as he is also to receive, celebrate and transmit the "pure deposit". This commits him to purifying the deposit of the inevitable waste matter it collects in order to transmit it in a more pure form than that in which he received it himself (a minister is necessarily involved in the *"perennis reformatio"* of the Church); it also obliges him to apply the Gospel, which is always identical with itself, to the very different historical, political, economic and social situations through which the Church passes on its pilgrimage.

This consent on the part of the minister to his ordination is of course not sufficient to justify it, and still less to be its basis.

Nevertheless it is constitutive of ordination, as the profession of faith is of baptism or the consent of the parties of marriage.

IV. The Function of the Community

The role of the assembly in an ordination is less clear. There are even a very few rare cases known in the Reformed Church of ordinations celebrated in the presence of ministers alone. I have been able to find very few texts which would indicate that at an ordination the Church itself exercised a sort of "priesthood" by offering one of its members to the service of God; in fact, the idea that the minister is taken from among the flock to become as it were its spokesman and agent is hardly to be found. The minister is much more a man God gives to the Church than a man the Church offers to God. That is why there is also no thought of basing the ministry on the "universal priesthood" or even of making a close connection between the two. If the Church has a fundamental role in relation to the ministry, it is in being the sphere in which it is exercised; it is also in the possibility the Church has of saying a word which may be decisive when a minister becomes the minister of this or that congregation; no one can usurp the ministry or thrust himself into it simply through his own desire to exercise it—a man is "called and elected by ecclesiastical and legitimate election", in the words of the *Second Helvetic Confession*. The meaning of this is not so much that by ordination a man is delegated by the Church to do what, essentially, any believer would have the right to do, but the majority leave to the minister for the sake of order; this election shows, rather, that this minister is *received* by this congregation as a gift of God's grace to it—again in the words of the *Confession*—"to keep it in the way of life". Election is an act of acceptance rather than an act of delegation, and if such an election is necessary for the normal exercise of a ministry, that is not because it authorizes it in the strict sense; election rather reveals the portion of the people of God in which the man chosen must show that he rightly bears the title of *Verbi Divini Minister*.[9]

[9] In the beginning, election, ordination and installation were sometimes identical, and there are cases which remind one of some episcopal elections

V. The Current Problem

If, after these historical summaries, we want to deal with the problem as it presents itself today, we need, in my view, to say two things.

We should begin by recognizing the close connection between the Reformed doctrine of the ministry and the dominant "Catholic" tradition on the doctrine of the episcopacy. This should be the starting-point for any discussion of the difficult problem of the ministry between Catholics and members of the Reformed churches.

Secondly, we should point to the indisputably "sacramental" character of ordination, even if the Reformed Church does not include it among the sacraments strictly so called. It has an honourable tradition going back to the apostles; it takes place in the Church and for the Church; it is presided over by someone authorized for the task; it is accompanied by the visible sign of the laying on of hands; the Holy Spirit is invoked upon a man whose life is being dedicated to the service of God, who is being given the right to become, through the word, the sacraments and the keys, an administrator of the mysteries of God and is being given a place in the college of those who, as successors of the apostles, have the task of gathering together and building up the Church in the time which separates Pentecost from the Parousia. If ordination is not a sacrament for the Reformed churches, this discriminatory ruling is due primarily to a definition of sacrament so restrictive that it left no room for ordination. The question at issue in this context between "Catholics" and "Reformed" seems to me to be not so much whether ordination is or is not essential to the life of the Church, but whether it is possible to agree on a definition of sacrament which will allow institutions and events other than baptism and the Eucharist to be called sacraments. If such an agreement were reached, it seems

---

in the early Church; but in general it is a case not so much of the Church *giving* itself ministers as of *receiving* them. Theologically, the relations between ordination and election in the Reformed Church are comparable to those between ordination and canonical mission in the Roman Catholic Church.

to me certain that ordination to the ministry would be counted as a sacrament.

Translated by Francis McDonagh

3. A Catholic Reply

Jos Lescrauwaet

IN ANY attempt to recognize each other's offices, the Protestant theologian cannot automatically accept the Catholic view of a "sacrament of ordination". He invariably wants the Catholic to justify this claim by establishing its biblical foundation. He is also afraid of clericalism and suspicious of a possibly unbiblical sacralization of office in the Church. The Catholic theologian must keep this Protestant fear in mind and not be content with a simple textual reference. The biblical foundation of office in the Catholic Church calls for deep reflection about the Church as such, which I would define as characterized by faith in the historical Jesus who, as the living Christ, unites those who believe in him with himself and with each other through the Spirit. I hope that this will provide a common point of departure for a joint ecumenical search.

I. JESUS' COMMUNICATION OF HIMSELF AS THE CHRIST

The bond between the historical Jesus as the still living Christ and those who believe in him is expressed in the Church in the typically Christian phenomenon of the preaching of the Gospel and in those evangelical actions which have come to be called sacraments. In preaching, we are not simply told about the historical Jesus. The word of the living Christ is also made real in the world of today. Similarly, the sacraments are a self-communication not only of the historical Jesus, but of the Lord living here and now. The word and the sacrament are not simply instruction; they also arouse faith. They do not simply enable us to understand; they also call for a positive response. The living Christ uses them as his means of communication.

Through these means of communication the Lord creates a lasting community, a bond between himself and those who believe, and between the believers themselves. The mission of the historical Jesus was to bring men together. So, too, the word of the living Christ is a "gathering" word and his sacrament is a communal celebration. Christians do not form his community simply by making the event of the historical Jesus psychologically present or by passing on his ideas. They become a community by collectively experiencing their bond in faith with him who "always lives" (Heb. 7. 25). The Church does not live simply by a purely intentional association with Christ, but in a real relationship with him "who was and is and is to come" (Apoc. 4. 8). The living Christ is the continuous source of life in the community of the Church in which he abides. The Church is his body, filled with his Spirit. It is in and through this community that he makes himself present not only to those who already believe, but also to those who do not yet know him, in the time between the first Easter and his Second Coming, when his mission will be accomplished.

To the extent that it is obedient to its vocation, the Church makes the saving actions of the Lord and the now unseen Christ himself present among men. The Lord himself speaks through the Church so long as it is faithful to its task of preaching. He incorporates new members into his body and fills them with his Spirit when the Church baptizes them in his name. He himself creates the community, the bond between himself and those who believe, and between all believers, whenever the Church celebrates the Last Supper.

The Church, then, is the sign and the instrument of Christ's saving activity. It is the "sacrament of Christ"—the Second Vatican Council made use of a patristic understanding of the mystery of the Church in the Constitution on the Church: "Rising from the dead, Christ has sent his lifegiving Spirit among the disciples; through the Spirit he has established his Body, which is the Church, as the universal sacrament of salvation."[1]

[1] *Lumen Gentium*, 48; see also 1 and 9.

II. In the Service of Christ's Communication of Himself

In the strict sense, of course, the Church in its totality does not preach, baptize, or celebrate the Lord's Supper. In each case, an individual does this as a task that he has received from Christ through the Church. This is not simply a question of practical necessity. The basic structure of the Church is revealed in this preaching and ministry of one individual "face to face" with his fellow believers. The Church is seen to be not just a corporation of people disposed towards Christ, but the body of Christ, the sacrament in which their salvation is achieved by God's initiative in Christ.

Our faith is directed towards God's coming to us in the life and work of the historical Jesus who is now our living Lord. It is a response to his saving acts, once performed in history and now carried out supratemporally in the Spirit. But Jesus' historical acts are revealed and made present in this supratemporal activity of the living Christ in the Spirit. The Church is the body of Christ whenever it makes Christ present, in its typically ecclesial activities, as the one Head.

From the very beginning, then, Christians regarded themselves as a community of brothers set up by Christ himself. Only those whom God had "appointed in the Church" (1 Cor. 12. 28-29) were teachers, healers, and so on. In the first place, the apostles were accepted as sent by Christ. Then the elders appointed by the apostles came to be regarded as "guardians" appointed by the Holy Spirit "to feed the Church of the Lord" (Acts 20. 28). Paul, for example, sent Timothy to Corinth and told the community there to treat him well and with respect, "for he is doing the work of the Lord, as I am" (1 Cor. 16. 10). The various ministries in the Church are Christ's "gifts" to his community "for building up the body of Christ" (Eph. 4. 11, 12). All the varieties of gifts and ministries (1 Cor. 12. 28) come from God and are created by him.

There is a difference between the apostles as the founder-members of the Church and their collaborators and those who came later as teachers, healers, and so on. The latter are bound to the testimony of the apostles and to the basic structure of the Church. What was of paramount importance to the apostles was their direct contact with the Lord whom they met and knew as the one who had risen from the dead, and their task of expressing the mystery of Christ within the community of Christ. Jesus has not communicated himself as the living Christ to successive generations by means of new revelations, but by means of the apostolic testimony in the power of his Spirit.

It is clear, then, that the mission of the apostles grounds the other ministries and determines their character. According to the Constitution on the Church, "This divine mission, entrusted to the apostles by Christ, is going to last until the end of the world, since the Gospel which they have to transmit is the principle of all life for the Church for all time".[2]

The most important characteristic of this eschatological mission is that it points to the permanent and absolute place of the one who sent the apostles, who did not found the Church themselves, but in the name of Christ. He is the Head, the vital, dynamic principle of the identity of the Church. He himself preaches, baptizes, breaks bread and is present among "all nations" and "to the close of the age" (Matt. 28. 20), but he does all this by means of his apostles. The Lord himself reveals himself, in their activity, as "*the* apostle" sent by God (Heb. 3. 1) and as "*the* episkopos" of all believers (1 Pet. 2. 25). The apostles, their collaborators and those who are active in the context of and in the extended sense of this apostolic mission have therefore to be regarded as instruments of God, servants of Christ and instruments of his Spirit (see, for example, 1 Cor. 4. 1; 12. 4, 6).

III. The Sacrament of Ministry

Christ's permanent presence "face to face" with the Church, and its continued existence, are guaranteed by the fact that he is its Head. He is behind all its charismata, including those of the apostles. It is possible to speak of a sacramental character inherent in the charisma of office, in so far as this saving reality is expressed in the community.

The word "sacrament" is, of course, not used in the New Testament in the sense in which we understand it, but certain

[2] *Lumen Gentium*, 20.

actions were experienced as saving actions in the primitive Church. A person was included among the community of believers by being baptized, and later he would regularly take part in the Lord's Supper. Similarly, a man who was called to the ministry in the same community would be appointed by the laying on of hands and by prayer, as a gesture of conferring office (see Acts 6. 6; 13. 3; 1 Tim. 4. 14; 2 Tim. 1. 6). These ministries were seen to be as much effective expressions of Christ's presence in his community as baptism or the Eucharist.

As far as we know, Augustine was the first to speak of a "sacrament of ordination". By this, he meant one of those celebrations in the whole Church by which the Lord "has bound together the community of his new people, sacraments, few in number, easy to administer, but full of meaning, like baptism and the partaking of Christ's body and blood and all that Scripture mentions".[3] When the Church's understanding of sacramentality had developed, in the Middle Ages, to the point where seven sacraments were accepted, one of these was ordination. Peter Damian regarded it, together with baptism and the Eucharist, as one of the "three most important sacraments".[4]

In the later Middle Ages, however, the Church's understanding of itself as a community declined and the sacraments came to be seen more as individual means of grace rather than as effective signs of grace for the building up of the Church. The fundamental conception of the Church as the body of Christ and the sacraments as the signs of Christ's effective presence in the Church were not seriously considered by the Council of Trent, with the result that post-Tridentine theology throws little light on the sacrament of ordination.

It is only as a consequence of the renewal of biblical and patristic studies and the resulting understanding of the Church as the active sign of God's saving activity in Christ that this sacrament, together with baptism and the Eucharist, has been placed once again in its original context. The people of God are made into the community of Christ's Church, in which Jesus calls men together, sanctifies them and sends them out again into

---

[3] *De baptismo*, 1, 1, 2 (PL, 43, 109); *De bono coniugali*, 24, 32 (PL, 40, 394), *Ep.* 54, 1 (PL 33, 200).
[4] *Liber gratissimus*, 9 (PL, 145, 109).

the world, in a visible and functional manner, by the sacrament of ordination.

What does this sacramental ordination signify for the one who has been ordained to office in the Church? It means that he can be sure of the help of Christ in his ministry. It also means that he will be so involved with the saving reality of the Church that he will receive a special personal grace as a member of Christ's body. What, finally, does it signify for his fellow believers? It means that they too will receive grace by virtue of the charisma of his office, strengthened by the faith of the whole community.[5]

Translated by David Smith

[5] Very similar ideas have been developed by the Lutheran theologian E. Fincke in the collection *Das Amt der Einheit* (Stuttgart, 1964), pp. 79–134.

Hervé-Marie Legrand

The "Indelible" Character and the Theology of Ministry

I. The Controversy about "Character"

THE Council of Trent defined what is known in Roman Catholic sacramental theology as an "indelible character". At the seventh session of Trent, a definition was issued which has received no dogmatic codicil since then: "If anyone says that in the three sacraments of baptism, confirmation and orders, there is not imprinted in the soul a character, that is, a certain spiritual and indelible sign, from which it follows that they cannot be repeated, let him be anathema (*signum quoddam spirituale et indelebile, unde ea iterari non possunt*" (can. 9; Denz. 852).

The doctrine of the indelible character therefore applies to baptism and confirmation as much as to the sacrament of orders. In addition, can. 4 of the twenty-third session, concerning ordination, does not go beyond a reaffirmation that this sacrament imprints a character, without adding any particular reason, apart from the parallel with baptism and confirmation. (Denz. 964.)

1. *A Paradox*

There are numerous investigations and publications on the subject of the character of orders.[1] Yet hardly any interest is shown in that of baptism or confirmation. Why is ordination

[1] Among the attempts to reinterpret the notion of "character", see: R. J. Bunnik, *Dienaren van het aggiornamento* (Nijmegen and Utrecht, 1967); J. Flamand, "Réflexions pour une intelligence renouvelée du caractère sacerdotal", *Le Prêtre, hier, aujourd'hui, demain* (Paris, 1970); J. Moingt, "Caractère et ministère sacerdotal", *Recherches de Sc. Rel.*, 56 (1968),

singled out for this special treatment as if it were not but one part of the whole question of the indelible character? This paradox admirably illustrates the nature of the controversy: the primary and exclusive preoccupation is not a thesis of sacramental theology, but a search for a rectification of the theology of the presbyteral office.

Objections are increasingly raised nowadays against the "indelible" character as an "axis" for such a theology, in the sense of a individually possessed power, with no intrinsic reference to any actual community. For twenty years, pastoral thought, study of the origins, and ecumenism, have favoured a quite different approach which starts with the actual, wholly sacerdotal and apostolic community, within which and for which the instituted ministry, among other offices, is exercised.

These two views are often felt to be antagonistic, to the extent, indeed, that once a theologian's standpoint on the connection between the ministry and the community is known, it is possible to predict with assurance his view of the question of character: if he starts with the community, he will probably not attach much importance to the indelible character, and will, in fact, try to minimize the importance of this doctrinal point.

2. A Danger of Ideologization

Hence the question of the indelible character runs the risk of being treated only in terms of the actual functions of ministry. One must be aware of this ideologization of the discussion. It is epistemologically questionable to try to identify a doctrine with the consequences derived from it—perhaps wrongly. And it is difficult to see how a refusal to analyse the theory-practice relationship could justify examination of only the empirical role of a doctrine. For example: the fact that Mary's virginity is taken by many Christians to be some kind of a statement about sex (whereas its proper location is in Christology) is no reason for ignoring it. Discussion of the doctrine demands analysis of the role or roles that can play.

pp. 563-9; E. Schillebeeckx, *Theologische Peiligen*, IV (Bilthoven, 1969); P. Schoonenberg, "Quelques réflexions sur le sacrement de l'ordre, en particulier sur le caractère sacramental, *Bull. d'infor. de l'Instit. pour l'entr'aide sacerdotal. en Europe*, 2 (1968), pp. 59-62.

3. Methodology

As the previous example suggests, epistemologically it is just
as impermissible to confound a doctrine with one of its effects as
to treat its possible effects by preterition. The golden rule is to
shun both confusion and separation. Otherwise, as in the present
debate, ideology will prevent progress. Some, as a result of confusion, tend to disqualify the possible truth of the doctrine in the
name of its unwonted ecclesiological consequences; others, as a
result of separation, tend to isolate this point from other elements
of the theology of ministry. Luther may be seen as an example of
the first attitude. Because of the importance of his interpretation,
and in order to stress the ecclesiological nature of the debate between the churches on this subject, it is worth re-reading his
critique of "character" in the *De Capitivitate Babylonica*.[2] His
first concern is the community: the character identified in the
sacrament of orders is, for him, "the most proficient instrument
for consolidating all the deformations introduced into the
Church... the way by which Christian brotherhood has been
lost".[3] Seeing only the ecclesiological consequences of the doctrine
("clerical tyranny"), Luther did not bother his head any further
about any possible content of truth in it.

For their part, the "defenders" of the actuality of "character"

---

[2] "...have conceived characters, which they have attributed to their
sacrament [of order] and which are said to be communicated as indelible
to those who are ordained accordingly... they have sought to affirm a
distinction between clergy and laity more definite than that between heaven
and earth, thus showing unbelievable contempt for the grace of baptism
and heaping up confusion for the evangelical communion. In this way there
began that detestable tyranny of clergy over laity.... For, according to the
Scriptures, what we call a priesthood is only a ministry, and I do not see
why he who has been ordained priest cannot become a layman once again.
He differs from the layman only by virtue of his ministry, and it is so little
impossible to be deprived of a ministry... as one may still see this measure
being applied to guilty priests, for this invention of the indelible character
has already been rendered derisory. I concede that the pope imprints this
character of which Christ knows nothing, and that the priest marked in
this way is the perpetual slave and captive not of Christ but of the pope.
If this sacrament and this invention perish, the papacy itself, with all its
characters, will find it difficult to exist, but for all of us that will be the
return to that joyous liberty, by virtue of which we are all equal" (*De capt.
babyl.* W.A. 6, pp. 562-3, 567).

[3] *Ibid.*, p. 564.

do not hesitate to make it fundamental to the presbyterate. But does this allow respect for the hierarchy of truths? Is this not something like making limbo or original sin the decisive element in baptism? By ignoring the ecclesiological dimension of the problem, such proponents of "character" are, of course, far from taking a disinterested attitude to ecclesiology. They are content to opt, more or less consciously, for an ecclesiology that suits their case. They see in the debate something other than respect for an abstract truth: the very trustworthiness of the priesthood is thought to be bound up with the indelible character. Should it disappear, so they say, it will not be long before the requests for reduction to the laity rapidly increase. The fear expressed justifies, in the eyes of opponents, a denunciation of the "character" as an "instrument of repression in the hands of the hierarchy". In this way both sides are prevented from conducting a measured theological discussion.

4. First Conclusion

In order to remain epistemologically appropriate in such a context, reflection on the nature of the "character" has to avoid this threat of ideologization by trying to weigh separately the dogmatic force of the pronouncements of the magisterium and the ecclesiological consequences drawn from them. It must also relate these two approaches, while respecting their relative autonomy.

This article is written in such a spirit, with the hope not of elucidating the whole problem (which is the most obscure of the theology of the ministry), but of showing that when it is examined with sufficient rigour, it need not be a factor to divide Christians.

II. The Actual Dogmatic Weight of the Teaching on the Indelible Character

Since it is impossible to review here all the Church's teaching relative to the question of "character", I shall restrict myself to an attempt to answer two questions: (a) What was defined? (b) Were these definitions of faith?

1. What was defined?

Since Vatican II was content to recall that priests are "marked with a special character", we have to go back to Trent to find the dogmatic teaching in complete form. Trent wished to answer the Lutheran denial of "character" in the belief that it was tantamount to a denial of the belief of the Catholic Church: it therefore reaffirmed the "impression in the soul", by means of the sacrament of orders, of an indelible spiritual sign. Thanks to the Council documents, it is possible to rediscover the precise implications of such a proposition.

(a) Trent merely affirms the existence of the character and expressly renounces any affirmation as to its nature. In a detailed study, J. Galot has shown the many contrasted medieval views of "character".[4] Thomists and Scotists were seriously divergent on this point. The ontological interpretation of character was far from unanimous. Olivi saw only a juridical relation between Christ and the priest. Durand de Saint-Pourçain saw a mere relation of reason.[5] Faced with this situation, Trent "wanted expressly to avoid any determination regarding the nature of the character and the fact that it is not reducible to the external gesture of the rite, as held by, for example, St Augustine".[6]

(b) Trent avoids going into detail about the connection of the character with the non-repeatability of the sacrament. A first recension explained indelibility as a "reason for which they cannot be repeated (cuius ratione ea iterari non possunt)." Refusing to conclude the debate, the Fathers substituted for this formula (which they rejected) a vaguer unde, which was already in the Armenian decree.[7] The Council wanted to record the practice of non-repetition of certain sacraments, or to see the existence of the character as the impossibility of repeating them. By comparing the doctrine and the canon, it can clearly be seen that Trent

[4] J. Galot, La nature du caractère sacramentel. Etude de théologie médiévale (Bruges, 1957).

[5] Ibid., p. 224.

[6] N. Haring, "St Augustine's use of the word 'Character' ", Med. Studies, 14 (1952), pp. 79–97, shows that he never conceived character as a sign "in the soul". For Cyprian, on leaving the office one ceases to be a priest, cf. P. van Beneden, "Het sacramenteel karakter ven de ambsverlening", Tidjsch. voor Theol., 8 (1968), pp. 140–54.

[7] Conc. Trid., V, 984–92; cf. J Galot, op. cit., p. 224.

did not wish to affirm a consequential link between the impression of the character and the impossibility of the priest becoming a layman once again.

(c) Trent made no distinction between the character of orders and that of the other sacraments. It offered no foundation for any attempt to understand the character of orders in functional terms while that of baptism and that of confirmation would be ontological. This problem is alien to Trent, since it does not exclude the possibility that the character may be no more than a relation of reason.

To sum up: Just as someone who has been confirmed can no longer be considered as never having been confirmed, so one who has been ordained. The ordination produces a permanent result: in connection with (but one refuses to say—because of) this fact, a minister cannot be ordained! In short, the content of the most official Catholic teaching on the character is singularly precise and circumscribed. But is it a definition of faith?

2. Is it a Definition of Faith?

In order to find out whether the Tridentine Fathers saw the character as a revealed truth, one has to try to estimate their intention and the value of the "anathema sit" which closes their definition.

(a) Their intention was to reaffirm the doctrine of the Armenian decree. The existence of the character was not defined in terms of a scriptural or patristic argumentation. Impossible on such a level, the agreement of the Fathers could only reaffirm the declarations of the magisterium (the Majores; the Decree to the Armenians). It is abundantly clear that they reproduced this second decree without adding anything to it. And it is certain that the Decree to the Armenians has not the value of a doctrinal analysis, since it does not include definitions which are binding upon faith.[8] It must therefore be decided whether Trent, in sanctioning its affirmations with an anathema, intended to go beyond this level of affirmation.

(b) The anathema of Trent does not mean a definition of

---

[8] J. de Guibert, "Le décret de Florence pour les Arméniens. Sa valeur dogmatique", Bull. de litt. ecclés., 10 (1919), pp. 81–95; 150–62; 195–215: who cites Cardinals Gasparri and van Rossum in the same sense.

faith. Let us consult the experts on this point: the presence of the *anathema* is not a certain and sure sign of the intention to issue a definition of faith.[9] The further decisions of the papal magisterium confirm this.[10]

(c) The teaching of Trent in regard to the character therefore represents an ordinary teaching of the Latin Church of the fifteenth to the twentieth centuries. The doctrine of the "character", which was unknown in this precise form to the first thousand years of Christianity, was never accepted by the Eastern Church—apart from a few Latinized Russians at one particular moment in time;[11] the rarity of the designation of ordination as *sphragis* by the Greek Fathers explains this. The doctrinal status of "character" is that it is an ordinary teaching only of the Latin Church—and in the modern age.

3. Second Conclusion

In regard to the rules for interpretation of dogmatic texts found in can. 1323, art. 3, according to which "the definitions, even the most solemn, must be interpreted in the strictest possible sense, there being defined therein only that which authority manifestly wished to define," one would be expressly disloyal to the intentions of the doctrinal authority of the Catholic Church were one to consider the doctrine of the "character" as a dogma.

III. CHARACTER AND THE THEOLOGY OF MINISTRY

The dogmatic content of "character" really seems too inadequate, once one has appraised it proficiently, to serve as a valid

[9] Cf. R. Favre, "Les condamnations avec anathème", *Bull. de litt. ecclés.*, 47 (1946), especially pp. 232–41; and 48 (1947), pp. 31–46; and particularly, among P. Fransen's works, "Le concile de Trente et le sacerdoce", in *Le Prêtre, foi et contestation* (Paris, 1970), pp. 106–42, and "Wording en strekking van de canon over het merkteten te Trente", *Bijdragen*, 32 (1971), pp. 2–34.

[10] A valuable study by J. B. Umberg: "Die Bewertung der Tridenter Lehren durch Pius VI", *Scholastik*, 4 (1929), pp. 402–9.

[11] Cf. M. Jugie, "La doctrine du caractère sacramentel dans l'Eglise grécorusse", *Echos d'Orient*, 27 (1928), pp. 17–23; B. Schultze, "Die byzantinisch-slawische Theologie über den Dienst der Laien in der Kirche", *Ostkirch. Stud.*, 5 (1956), pp. 243 ff.

"axis" for a developing theology of ministry. Nevertheless, such a procedure has been followed since the thirteenth century, and above all since Trent. It is possible only to summarize the results of such a choice here—it was both the reflection and the cause of the rupture between the ministry and the community.

(a) Since the notion of "character" focused attention on the person of the minister, it made it more difficult to see the *object* of the ministry. When thought on this subject starts from the concept of "character", it is no longer based on a theology of *ministry*, that is, of service to the people of God, but on a theology of the cult: the priest becomes the one who is personally empowered to offer the Eucharist. This perspective, which goes with absolute ordinations (without ministry) and private masses, puts the person of the priest at the forefront, to the detriment of the object of the ministry. The serious imbalances which result can be seen in the replacement of the ecclesiological determination of the presbyteral ministry by the "ontological" qualification of the priest. The indelibility of the "character" reinforces this removal of the ministry from its proper location. Henceforth the person of the minister is more determinative than the choice of the communty and the charism of the Spirit.

We all know how much the question of the permanence of the priesthood depends on this mentality. If the will of the ordinand counts for more than that of the community and the action of the Spirit, it is clear that priests will leave the ministry (or will be reduced to the lay state) for invalid reasons, other than loss of faith or unsuitability. The idea of an ordination for a limited period derives from the same mentality: it runs the risk of delaying the urgently required reform of orders.

(b) The "character" has accentuated the difference between clergy and laity. The fact of "character" was used to consolidate the "superiority" of clergy to laity. It has also been seen as the basis for their special way of life.[12] This doctrine has helped to split the unity of the *ecclesia*.

(c) By emphasizing the notion of power, "character" has

---

[12] J. Galot, "Sacerdoce et célibat", *Nouv. Rev. Théol.*, 86 (1964), pp. 116–124: "Character . . . the basis of priestly celibacy". J. Maritain, "A propos de l'école française," *Rev. Thom.*, 71 (19971), pp. 463–79, demystifies this theology of "character".

devalued that of service. As J. Lécuyer says, "all the Thomist theology of order centres upon the idea of transmitted 'power', and not primarily on that of a gift of the Holy Spirit in view of a particular ministry within the Church, as in the patristic period".[13] Is it surprising that in this non-pneumatological universe the notion of service became blurred and the clergy self-sufficient? The doctrine of "character" goes with a break between ministers and community, and in fact served to reinforce that break.[14]

IV. CAN THE DOCTRINE OF CHARACTER BE PASTORALLY USEFUL AND ECUMENICALLY ACCEPTABLE?

Why has a doctrine that is so weak dogmatically played such a considerable (and often questionable) ecclesiological role? The ecumenical difficulty refers not so much to the dogma itself as to the pastoral consequences. Only by interpreting "character" in the scriptural sense of charism can one satisfy both pastoral and ecumenical demands. To interpret "character" as meaning only that ordination really took place is to minimize its implications. It also affects the individual ordained. But how, other than under the form of the charism received in ordination according to 2 Tim 1. 6? Within this necessarily ecclesiological, pneumatological framework, the charism would seem to be conferred in view of the ministry, in the diversity of services which constitute the community. Within this framework some commentators would think it is better to abandon the term "indelible character". There are in fact no inconveniences and only advantages in speaking as Scripture speaks. While in communion with other ministers, a community receives its own minister; priests know that their trustworthiness does not depend on them alone, for through their ordination they have personally received a lasting gift from God. Does not this characterize the only point of the doctrine of "indelible character" to which the Catholic faith is really committed? Understood in this way, the doctrine cannot be a factor of division among Christians.

Translated by Verdant Green

[13] J. Lécuyer, *L'ordre* (Paris, 1968), p. 170.
[14] Cf. Y. Congar, *L'Eglise de Saint Augustin à l'époque moderne* (Paris, 1970), for the period which started with the Gregorian reform.

How can we arrive at a Theological and Practical, Mutual Recognition of Ministries?

1. *An Orthodox Reply*

Boris Bobrinskoy

THIS is no longer an academic problem of canon law, but an increasingly urgent existential question. We reckon upon, or at least hope for, a positive answer to the question of the recognition of orders. Hence the formulation is not "Can we...?" but "How can we...?" The sense of the question is therefore one of theological principles and practical modes of recognition.

Orthodox Christians are not the only ones who are asked to reply. For this is really an inquiry—a large-scale ecumenical survey. It is concerned with all the Christian denominations, which are to give their answers in general or particular terms according to the specific importance of general principles or special cases (churches in dialogue or ministers seeking reintegration, etc.).

An Orthodox reply ought really to be based on an Orthodox consensus regarding the theology of the ministry. This consensus would also take into account any future decision about the "recognition" of the sacraments as administered by separated Christians.

The practical difficulties vary according to special and individual cases. Here the principle of sacramental economy finds application. This means that the recognition of any particular ministry cannot occur in the Orthodox Church apart from a procedure firmly committed to Orthodoxy.

Even though the act of recognition of ministries must occur within a process of unification, this does not mean that Orthodoxy definitively rejects or negates non-Orthodox ministries. The Church's judgment is always existential, in dialogue, and

63

does not correspond to a formal canonical *satisfecit*, or to a rejection pure and simple of the ecclesiality of a Christian denomination. If the Holy Spirit is the inspirer of the unity of the Church, he is also the one who "always cures weaknesses and supplies deficiencies" (Orthodox liturgy of ordination).

The attitude of Orthodoxy towards the sacramentality of separate confessions should be primarily a prophetic attitude of humble spiritual discernment and pastoral discretion; it necessarily includes a dimension of hope and of inward understanding of the living and charismatic reality of the separate churches and a serious confrontation with the particular doctrine of the Church and of the sacraments, and the precise intention governing ordination to the ministry. "A dynamic attitude on the part of Orthodoxy", says N. Nissiotis, "prevents us from locating any ecclesiological fact '*extra ecclesiam*'" ("Temoignage et Service de l'Eglise une par l'Orthodoxie", in *Contacts*, 1969, nos. 38–9, p. 201). The primary and essential "ecclesiological fact" is that a Christian community is capable of fulfilling the function of priestly mediation between God and the world and that it features the fruits of the light, "all that is good and right and true" (Eph. 5. 9). To instigate, encourage and recognize these fruits of the Spirit is to recognize and give thanks to God for "whatever is true, whatever is honourable, whatever is just, whatever is pure, whatever is lovely, whatever is gracious... and [then] the God of peace will be with you" (Phil. 4. 8–9).

I. Orthodox Theology of Ministries

1. *The Eucharist and Orders*

Only on the basis of the eucharistic nature of the Church is it possible to comprehend the role and proper nature of the ministry (and of the laity) in the life of the ecclesial community. The Eucharist, as the primary and constitutive fact of the Church, determines the priestly ministry. It is inseparable from the communitarian actuality of the Church, from the people as a whole in the eschatological community. This royal priesthood of the Church signifies a mediation of salvation between God and the world, in which the Church continues and reveals the royal, priestly and prophetic mediation of Christ himself, in the pentecostal diversity of human individuals reborn through baptism, consecrated to the priestly mediation of the Church by the chrism of confirmation, nourished and maintained by the Eucharist in this situation of crucifying tension, of being an eschatological sign between God and the world.

The ministerial or hierarchical priesthood tends, within the Church, to the permanence of mediation "for the life of the world", to the belief and cohesion of communities, to the "edification" of individuals, to the services of the word and the sacraments. Like the royal priesthood, the hierarchial ministry is defined on the basis of the ministry of Christ, the only "high priest of future benefits", the pastor and bishop of our souls, the apostle of the Faith, the servant of God and the servant of men, the liturgist of the word. The concept of the hierarchical ministry does not contradict this uniqueness and exclusiveness of Christ's, the sole mediator's, ministry. In its multiform diversity, the hierarchical ministry actualizes and reflects, within that time of the Spirit which is the Church, the unique and sufficient ministry of Christ.[1]

2. Diversity and Unity of Ministries

The work of the Holy Spirit is precisely to distribute the ministries, and to diversify them according to the needs of the Church, but always in relation to the unity of the ecclesial community. This is the meaning of the threefold hierarchy (bishop, presbyter, deacon), whose axis and source of unity is the historical episcopate, but each of whose three forms constitutes not only a formal and canonical step towards the higher orders, but a constant and necessary dimension of the unique and multiple hierarchical ministry which is always consecration (archiereus), fatherhood (presbyteros), service (diakonia). The work of the Holy Spirit would also consist in making this ministry an authentic, living and recognizable "reflection", which would correspond dynamically with the Prototype. Christ is always the

---

[1] This organic relation of hierarchical ministries has recently been stressed by J. Zizioulas in "L'Eucharistie: quelques aspects bibliques", in L'Eucharistie, ed. J. Zizioulas, J. M. R. Tillard and J. J. von Allmen (Tours, 1970), pp. 49–50.

origin of the priestly and diaconal vocation, both in the continuity of the apostolic and uninterrupted hierarchy and in the uniqueness of the individual vocation which, throughout the ages, derives from the living call of Jesus of Nazareth: "Follow me, and I will make you fishers of men" (Mt. 4. 19).

The Holy Spirit will always signify the truth of the personal vocation, i.e. the miracle of synergy, of man's response to the call of God, of man's ability to hear, recognize and welcome the word.

The Holy Spirit is therefore the one who distributes the ministries. There is no hierarchical ministry which is not pneumatic, and hence charismatic, by nature and vocation: that is, which does not depend on the pouring-forth of the Spirit. The consecratory epiclesis of the ordination service recalls the dynamism of vocation, the need for the renewal of the priestly judgment of God by which it is marked.

3. The Validity or Truth of Ministries

This enables ordination and priesthood to be freed from an "objectifying" and "factistic" sacramentalist conception which would treat ordination (or baptism, or eucharistic communion) as a sacrament "in itself", according to its possession of the norms and marks of objective validity. The Church (and the Holy Spirit in it) is the sole judge, not only of formal validity, but of the sacramental, charismatic, living "truth" of the sacramental mysteries.

The sacrament of orders, just like baptism or the Eucharist, is inseparable from the entire ecclesiality which it manifests and protects. This ecclesiality signifies a global relation of the hierarchical ministry to the eucharistic community, to its profound life, tradition and holiness. This ecclesial context has several, complementary dimensions.

(a) The hierarchical ministry exists in a state of creative tension in relation to a local community, by virtue of the internal collegiality of the community.

(b) It is horizontal, ensuring the reciprocal communion of local communities in space, in the diocese, in the local church, in the universal Church, by virtue of episcopal collegiality, culminating in the Council.

(c) It is vertical, being located in the charismatic continuity of the apostolic succession, which is expressed by the episcopate (which it guarantees), by virtue of historical collegiality. For the Orthodox, the apostolic succession is one of the aspects of the continuity of the Church, which has, however, too often been separated from the total context of the life of the Church and included in an exclusively institutional and legal framework, guaranteeing securely the "validity" of hierarchical orders, independently both of the faith of the individual and of that of the Church (doctrine), as well as of the entire life of the Church considered in the aspect of its collegiality.

Of course the bishop is the instrument for the transmission of the apostolic message and power, but the *"charisma veritatis certum"* (Irenaeus of Lyons, *Adv. Haer.*, IV, 11, 2), which is passed on to him in the laying on of hands, is manifested only in the local church and not above that level. The bishop is not alone: he is inseparable from his community, within which he acts, teaches and administers.

(d) Finally, it is direct, existing in a unique and inward relation of the eucharistic community with the divine life, inscribing the human collegiality in its source and foundation, the everlasting and perfect council of the Holy Trinity.

The bishop or the minister is therefore the sign and the representative of the entire eucharistic community in its unity, and in time and in space. This multi-dimensional collegiality of the hierarchy and of the people as a whole is the necessary condition for a horizontal collegiality of the episcopate, i.e. of an ecclesiology of communion and not of one of dependence and of power; and for a vertical collegiality of the apostolic succession of churches, eucharists, ministries, sanctity and faith: it is the totality of that living succession that the bishop represents in communion with the ecclesial people.

Recognition of ministries (or of sacraments, or of the doctrine taught) is in itself no more than the necessary and permanent exercise of this sacramental collegiality, in a charismatic discernment of the truth, grace, faith, and authenticity of the sacramental structures which are requisite for the mediation of the Church in the world.

II. THEOLOGICAL RECOGNITION OF MINISTRIES

1. *Unity of Sacraments*

Baptism, the Eucharist and the hierarchical ministry are inseparable elements of a unique and global ecclesial reality. To attempt to isolate one of these components as a minimal common denominator leads to an "anti-natural" sacramental dissection, and to a legal conception of the "validity" of sacramental acts considered "intrinsically" outside the global context of the faith, and of the living tradition and very life of the Church.

Christian baptism does not merely constitute the minimal common denominator for legal membership of the Church. It includes a promise and commitment here and now of fullness of faith and Christian life in the Church.

The ecumenical dialogue regarding "faith and constitution" is at present (and has been especially since Louvain 1971) concerned with an increasing consensus of the member churches of the C.O.E. (and of the Roman Catholic Church, which in the future will participate fully in the "faith and constitution" dialogue) on the meaning and content of baptism as the sacrament of the new birth in the Holy Trinity, within the ecclesial community. More and more, it would seem to be agreed that Christian initiation is a unique process in which the completion and finality of baptism are situated in the eucharistic communion (for children as for adults), within the framework of the eucharistic celebration presided over by the ordained minister. Consequently, the problem of the "validity" of sacraments tends increasingly to be considered in a universal and living manner, and not treated legalistically and piecemeal.

2. *Danger of Indifference*

Is it possible nowadays to go beyond this damaging reduction of the baptismal mystery to a legal and formal act; to escape this dilemma which forces us either automatically to accept participation in the Eucharist as deriving from baptism, even though it is not accompanied by a common confession of faith (Protestant attitude), or automatically to reject the baptism of other confessions (Greek Orthodox attitude)? I think that these two extreme views are located in the same complex of problems regarding the formal validity (or invalidity) of the sacraments "in themselves", either in an ecclesiology of the institutional type, where the hierarchy possesses, administers and distributes the sacraments, while protecting itself from "heterodoxy" by means of insurmountable canonical barriers, or in an ecclesiology of the "event" type, where any canonical limitation appears as an intolerable pressure on the freedom of the Spirit. In the most extreme forms of these attitudes, this "all or nothing" legalistic dilemma also compromises dialogue and ecumenical progress. It also displays a profound indifference towards the spiritual identity, faith and sacramental dynamism of separated Christians, and features a serious dichotomy of truth and life, to the detriment of the one or the other.

In the case of non-recognition of baptism, and consequently of all the sacraments (in particular, the Eucharist and orders), to start from the sole criterion of dogmatic truth and the common confession of faith sometimes indicates ignorance and indifference with regard to the ecclesial and spiritual identity of separated Christians, and an inability to discern the breath of the Spirit of unity of truth and life beyond the canonical limits of one historical church. The unacknowledged need for security leads to attitudes which may be defined as unyielding rejection and, ultimately, as serious injustice to the Holy Spirit.

The automatic and non-separate recognition of the baptism and ecclesial sacraments of separated Christians on the basis of the sole criterion of the existential experience of the actual life of the separate Christian communities can also display no less a degree of indifference to the faith as it is lived actually and historically in another ecclesial tradition. The "intrinsic" recognition of sacraments isolates these sacraments and cuts them off from all the fullness of faith, which becomes relative and secondary.

The liturgies of baptism, of the Eucharist and ordination contain a confession of faith which is neither formal nor external to the sacrament, but belongs to its very essence. Baptismal and eucharistic initiation is an entry and a progression into the trinitarian community which is the Church, in the "real presence" of the saints, of the mother of Jesus, of the angels, of the dead and the living. The hierarchical ministers are visible (not exclusive) signs of a full apostolic succession of the Church, of its uninterrupted doctrinal and charismatic tradition, of the perennial nature of the evangelical message in the sacred history of mankind. These ministers are in the Church (which is the permanent eucharistic assembly) as guardians of the faith and of communion.

3. Minimal or Full Recognition

To "recognize" the ordained minister of a church is necessarily to recognize its faith, doctrine, teaching, living witness of sanctity and love, and not merely the "validity" of an ordination or the historically continuous nature of a succession.

"Recognition" of the ministry therefore has to be a total and full recognition in a reciprocal creative tension of faith and life, of truth and sanctity, of the sacramental structures and the grace which grounds and gives them life. Of course, "apostolic" churches can ossify, can close in on themselves, forming a ghetto mentality in their dead tradition, without giving out any ray of light or any witness, without noticing that they have become "wretched, pitiable, poor, blind and naked" (Rev. 3. 17). Nevertheless, the sacramental and doctrinal structures are necessary. They are signs of faith: channels for the divine life and for salvation. But the Church *is not* the signs; it is, above all, the very life of God who pours himself forth and makes holy: the Holy Spirit who gives the Lord Jesus and who offers himself in communion, thus transforming and divinizing human nature and the cosmos itself.

4. Recognition—an Ecclesial Charism of Spiritual Discernment

Therefore I would say that the very idea of the "recognition" of ministries (and of sacraments) is inadequately construed with regard to its actual profundity. This recognition is a constant and necessary act of the "spiritual discernment" of the whole Church, which must "test the spirits to see whether they are of God" (Cf. 1 Cor. 12. 10; 1 Jn. 4. 1). The ultimate author as well as the supreme object of this discernment is the Holy Spirit in person, in whom resides the ultimate truth of the judgments of the Church.

But the charism of the diacrisis is both discernment and discretion, judgment and confidence. This kind of judgment may be formally truthful, yet lack discretion, tenderness and patience, and can do more harm than good, can harden or dishearten. Sacramental recognition is therefore a profoundly responsible and demanding course of action, a spiritual judgment of the Church which is itself subject to the judgment of the Spirit.

This "recognition" is always an attitude of edification, of "ecclesial" economy, of condescension or of fraternal reprimand, an ecclesial and sacramental (not egalitarian) affirmation of identity or of non-identity, or a decision to wait, or to give judgment in a spirit of confidence in the future and by recourse to the Holy Spirit.

Certain conditions are necessary for this ecclesial recognition: authenticity of doctrine (Trinity, redemption, Church, sacraments, Holy Scripture, anthropology, ministry, communion of saints), sacramental and liturgical forms, an ascetic discipline as a living and ideal programme of sanctity, and so on. These criteria for recognition can never be automatic grids standing for an historical tradition and applied (according to the letter of its structures and its language) in judgment on another tradition. Not the least of the characteristics of spiritual discernment is the ability to recognize in Christian traditions, beyond fixed forms and languages, the luminous countenance of redemption, the inward progression and slow convergence by way of the sovereign dynamism of the Spirit, towards unity and truth, towards an authentic and profound life in Christ.

The recognition of ministries and ecclesiality seem to me to be part of the ministerial charism of the episcopate and of councils, within the constant epiclesis of the Church. The use of this prophetic charism is difficult for the discerning practitioner, for he cannot escape the exercise of this judgment, which in fact rebounds upon him. It is difficult for those who submit to this judgment, because it necessarily means a call to a reformation in depth, to a "return" by way of an ecclesial metanoia towards a greater integrity of faith and life, of language and witness. The recognition of ministries and of sacraments is therefore a long process whose beginning we must all devoutly pray for, and whose accomplishment we must hasten to bring about. It tends towards the re-establishment of the communion of faith, of love, of life and of service. It implies gestures of reparation, of repentance, of unity, even to the extent of a sacramental laying on of hands, on condition that this act is lived beyond its formal and legal meaning as the "validation" of a rite—lived as a sign of the re-establishment of the full communion of faith and the sacraments.

III. Practical Recognition of Ministries

1. Bilateral Negotiations in Orthodoxy

The recognition of ministries is, in the actual situation of the divided churches, a long process coextensive with the recognition of the mutual sacramental authenticity of the communities concerned. This process is under way in all the churches, either in terms of private relations, or in official contacts or even negotiations between the churches. The Orthodox Church participates in the ecumenical movement, either in a general fashion, or by means of bilateral meetings and conversations with the non-Chalcedonic "Oriental" churches, with the Old Catholics, the Anglicans, the Roman Catholic Church, and the Lutherans.

These bilateral discussions form an occasion for an exchange of information on faith, liturgical structures, the state of theological controversy; they allow an assessment of the existing consensus, and of continuing points of difference. These conversations also stimulate theological dialogue and research towards a more complete agreement of faith. In none of these conversations is the problem of the formal recognition of the validity of ministries considered in a privileged manner; instead, the doctrines of ministry and forms of ordination are compared in the light of Orthodox faith and tradition as a whole.

The most positive and progressive example of these bilateral discussions, at the level of Orthodoxy as a whole, seems to me to be the dialogue between the Orthodox churches and the non-Chalcedonic Oriental churches. Four non-official meetings between Orthodox and "Oriental" theologians have taken place since 1964. Considerable positive results have been recorded in regard to the essential point of contention, which is Christological dogma.

These meetings between theologians prepared the ground for and made possible the official meeting of the inter-Orthodox dialogue commission with the non-Chalcedonic churches, which took place at Addis Ababa from 18 to 29 August. It is hoped that this assembly will lead to an official assessment of the results of theological meetings, which will make possible concrete decisions leading towards the re-establishment of eucharistic communion between the two families of churches of the East, while awaiting a total jurisdictional and canonical fusion.[2]

I find it difficult to prejudge the forthcoming development of the theological conversations between the Orthodox churches and the other Christian confessions. It must be remembered that, parallel to these bilateral discussions with the Orthodox, the Old Catholic churches, the Anglicans, the Roman Catholics, the Reformed churches, the Methodists, and so on, are engaged in various bilateral dialogues. These conversations denote an intensive theological activity regarding progressive doctrinal unification, at the risk sometimes of a widening of the breach separating them from the Orthodox. This concerns especially the question of the ordination of women to the priesthood, the adoption of which would become a new obstacle to unity with the Orthodox. There are also the Protestantizing tendencies in Roman Catholicism, or in Anglicanism, which lead to an atrophying of the cult of the saints, of the angels, of the mother of God, to a reduction of the three-stage hierarchical ministry (episcopate, presbyterate, diaconate) to an egalitarian structure, and to an impoverishment of the cultic and symbolic forms of the sacraments.

On the other hand, Orthodoxy can only rejoice at this common progress towards unity, even outside its own limits, to the extent that the traditional faith is not impoverished or sacrificed to unity. Orthodoxy cannot ignore the basic theological agreement existing between several non-Orthodox communions and leading to a more and more universal practice of intercommunion and mutual recognition of orders. It should even state firmly that where the prerequisite condition of unity of faith is present, reciprocal eucharistic communion is an urgent necessity.

Orthodoxy should constantly manifest its presence within this complex and general ecumenical conciliation, as a partner or witness, always applying the charism of discernment or dis-

---

[2] The results of the meeting are not known at the time of writing.

cretion in every situation or concrete problem of this process of theological fermentation. Orthodoxy is constantly affected by this progress towards unity. *Nostra res agitur.*

An actual example of this open and affectionate "attention" on the part of the Orthodox may be seen in the present theological discussions between the Anglicans and Methodists on the one hand, and the Anglicans and Roman Catholics on the other.

New ordination rites have been jointly worked out by the Anglicans and Methodists, in view of the possible union between the two churches. These sacramentaries emphasize the Anglican understanding of the ministry. A Roman Catholic study commission recently examined these new plans for union in some detail and stated that, despite a "non-Catholic" convergence towards unity, the new ordination rites of the scheme for union agreed substantially with what the Roman Church itself professed in regard to the ministry intended by the Lord.[3]

R. Tillard made a very detailed report for the Anglican-Roman Catholic International Commission, and brought out especially the common desire for faithfulness to "Catholic" tradition, while specifying that the points of convergence were not as yet sufficient to establish a profound and definitive consensus. A similar report should soon be available in regard to Orthodoxy and Anglicanism, and the Roman-Anglican dialogue should be taken into consideration.

IV. CONCLUSION

The question posed regarding the mutual recognition of ministries seems to me to accord only inadequately with the Orthodox theology of the ministry and the practical attitude of the Orthodox churches towards the separated communities.

Ordination and the ministry should correspond to the theological norms and traditional teaching of the Church: the relation of the ministry to the Church, the sacramental mediation of salvation in the local historical community, the apostolic succession by way of episcopal ordination, the traditional liturgy of ordination to the ministry.

[3] J. M. R. Tillard, "Catholiques romains et anglicans: l'Eucharistie", in *Nouvelle Revue Théologique*, Vol. 93, June–July 1971, p. 645.

The importance of the uninterrupted apostolic succession is generally underlined. If, in its official bodies, the Roman Catholic Church has until now denied the validity of Anglican orders and affirmed the break in the apostolic succession of the episcopate of the Church of England, the Orthodox churches have generally taken a much more refined standpoint in this regard (especially the Orthodox church of Rumania), while insisting on the ecclesiological context of the recognition of Anglican orders.

If, therefore, the doctrine of ministry recovers its primitive significance of sign and expression of ecclesial fullness, of bond and witness of the visible unity and permanence of the Church in time and space, of guarantor of faith and of the ecclesial *diakonia*, then the mutual recognition of ministries is a necessary stage in the quest for unity. But full ecclesial unity should tend, beyond a mutual recognition of orders, beyond a provisionally necessary pluralism of orders, to the unity of the hierarchical ministry of the one cup of the one, holy, catholic and apostolic Church.

Translated by John Griffiths

2. A Lutheran Reply
Ulrich Kühn

IT IS clear that the present situation in the Roman Catholic and the Lutheran Churches and their attitude with regard to office have to be discussed before any conclusions can be drawn as to how mutual recognition of each other's offices can be achieved. I will analyse the situation in the first section of this article and set out my conclusions in the second.

I. THE SITUATION

(a) The Roman Catholic Church has made an official pronouncement about this problem in the documents of the Second

Vatican Council and especially in the Decree on Ecumenism, in which it is said quite plainly that the Protestant churches lack the sacrament of ordination (*sacramenti ordinis defectus, Unitatis redintegratio*, 22). This refers primarily to episcopal consecration, by which the "fullness of the sacrament of ordination" is conferred (Dogmatic Constitution, *Lumen Gentium*, on the Church, 21), and which can only be transmitted "by a current of succession which goes back to the beginning" (*Lumen Gentium*, 20) that is, by the uninterrupted chain of episcopal laying on of hands since the time of the apostles. What lies behind the statement about the lack of ordination, however, is either that this chain has been interrupted in the Protestant churches or else, where this chain has been externally maintained, as in the case of the Swedish Lutheran and the Anglican churches, the form and the intention of the administration of the sacrament have not been preserved.[1] In the Roman Catholic view, then, all ordinations carried out in the Protestant churches are invalid. The most important consequence of this is that these churches have not preserved the original and complete reality (*substantia*) of the eucharistic mystery (*Unitatis Redintegratio*, 22). What is more, they also *de facto* reject the authentic teaching office of the Roman Catholic Church, with the result that they lack the instrument "of which God makes special use to protect the believing community from misinterpreting the meaning of scriptural revelation and to guarantee that community's proper understanding of the fundamental truths revealed in the Bible".[2]

The hope that lies behind these statements is certainly that the Protestant communities will submit to the authority of the legitimate hierarchy, allow their orders to be made valid by means of re-ordination, and thus be able to celebrate a true eucharist and preach authentically. It is only if they do this that they can be regarded as churches in the full sense by the Roman Catholic Church.

(b) According to the Lutheran confessional writings, the Church has a public "preaching office" or *ministerium ecclesiasticum* founded by God for the purpose of preaching the Gospel

---

[1] See *Lexikon für Theologie und Kirche*, 1[2], pp. 554 ff.

[2] J. Feiner, "Kommentar zum Oekumenismusdekret", *ibid.*, Supplementary Volume 2, p. 115.

and administering the sacraments (*Confessio Augustana*, 5). This one office can only be held by those on whom it has been duly conferred by the Church (*Conf. Aug.*, 14). The bishop, whose office is discussed in *Confessio Augustana*, 28, has the essential task, given him by God's law, of preaching. His office is, in other words, the preaching office outlined in articles 5 and 14 of the *Confessio Augustana*. In addition to equating the office of preaching with that of the bishop, however, article 28 of the *Confessio Augustana* also distinguishes between bishops and pastors and insists that the latter should obey the former.[3] The Lutheran view is that it is good church order (although it is a human right and not simply a necessity) that there should be bishops in the Church, performing, in a given district, functions of the one office such as safeguarding pure doctrine, excommunicating and ordaining and conferring the office of pastor on the pastors.[4] Unlike Luther,[5] Melanchthon was prepared to recognize the Pope if the latter had been ready to regard his primacy as a human right and "to accept the Gospel" (*Schmalk. Art.*, signature).

No definite ecclesiastical constitution is necessary as a criterion for being a church. According to article 7 of the *Confessio Augustana*, it is "sufficient for true unity among the Christian churches that there is harmony in preaching the Gospel according to pure reason and in administering the sacraments in accordance with God's word". This shows how freely the Lutheran Church interprets its legal structures. All that really matters is that the functions of office are suitably carried out. The person exercising this function should "do nothing at all to the word and the office commended by Christ, whoever is preaching and teaching must do it well", Melanchthon affirmed in the *Tractatus de potestate et primatu papae* (n. 28).

In the Lutheran collection of confessional writings, the Book of Concords, too, we read that the presence of the body and blood of Christ in the Lord's Supper does not depend on the

[3] For this identification of the two offices, see *Conf. Aug.*, 28, n. 30, Latin text: *episcopi seu pastores*; for the pastors' submission to the bishops, see *ibid.*, n. 22, German text; for both questions, see P. Brunner, "Vom Amt des Bischofs", in *Pro Ecclesia*, 1 (Berlin and Hamburg, 1962), pp. 235-92.

[4] P. Brunner, *op. cit.*, pp. 256 ff.

[5] *Schmalk. Art.*, Part II, Art. IV, n. 7 f. Luther's reason was that it served no useful purpose and was only confusing to create such a universal office.

personal merits of the office-bearer, but only on the correct use
of Christ's words (*Sol. Decl.*, VII, 78). We may therefore conclude that the Lord's Supper celebrated by a layman in accordance with the words of the institution of the sacrament would
be valid, even if not legitimate in accordance with church order.
Finally, the power to ordain is present wherever the Church is
and, in any borderline case, this is where two or three are gathered together in Jesus' name (*Tractatus*, 67 f.). It is clear, then,
that, in accordance with God's law, the Church insists no more
on a definite, legally established form of conferring office than
it does on a definite constitution. The Church is only really
apostolic when it bases itself on the *teaching* of the Apostles.

(c) In the context of a reciprocal recognition of offices, the
most striking factor to emerge from a comparison of the official
Catholic position and the official Lutheran position is the complete difference between the criteria applied. The criterion of
being a church is, on the one hand, only the suitable carrying
out of certain functions in accordance with God's law. On the
other hand, this criterion is above all the preservation of certain
legal structures of office and of handing on office as arranged by
God.

It is only possible for the Catholic Church to come to a recognition of office in the Lutheran Church on the basis of this second
criterion. There is, then, no question of a strictly mutual recognition, because the *satis est* of article 7 of the Lutheran *Confessio Augustana* ("It is sufficient for true unity among the Christian churches...") is completely opposed to the Catholic
criterion. The Lutheran *satis est* makes it possible for the
Lutheran Church to accept the Catholic hierarchy so long as the
Gospel is suitably preached. It also confronts the Church with
the task of never ceasing to look for the most useful legal structures for the gospels although these may be very varied, according to changing historical and geographical situations.

(d) These, then, are the official positions. They have, however, been greatly modified and developed in recent years by
theologians on both sides. The Catholic theologian Hans Küng,
for example, claims that the apostolic task of proclaiming the
Gospel is given to the whole Church and is accomplished in
the universal priesthood of all believers. The apostolic legality of

the special ministry of president of the Christian community is not, in Küng's view, bound to the chain of uninterrupted imposition of hands. He asks whether the validity of the eucharistic celebrations of those churches that are not within this chain of ordinations should not be judged differently and indeed more positively than they were judged at the Council. With regard to the office of Pope, as the "primacy of service of an individual in the Church", Küng believes that this should not be regarded as a criterion for where the Church is, nor as a dividing line, on the other side of which there can only be heterodoxy.[6]

Within the Lutheran Church, the discussion about office is based to a great extent on an exposition of the confessional writings. One of the problems considered is whether the ministry responsible for preaching the Gospel and dispensing the sacraments does not call for a greater diversity of form than the one office of pastor (as recognized by the Reformation) can provide. Expressed in another way, what Lutheran theologians are now considering is whether this "ministry" of *Conf. Aug.* 5 may perhaps only refer to certain functions which the Church has, according to God's law, to exercise. In other words, these functions may perhaps not be carried out in *one* concrete "office", but rather in a plurality of ministries within the Church. The fact that there were many different offices in the primitive church community plays a very important part in this debate.[7]

It cannot be denied that it is these and other recent developments in theological thinking about office in the Church, and above all those in Catholic circles, that have made it possible for Catholics and Lutherans in dialogue in the United States and elsewhere to achieve such remarkable results.[8] The North American theologians recommend that each Church should accept the other's office as valid and recognize the true presence of the body and blood of Christ in each other's Eucharist. The same

[6] H. Küng, *Die Kirche* (Freiburg, 1967), pp. 501 ff., 521, 562 (Eng. trans.: *The Church*, London, 1968).
[7] See U. Kühn, "Amt und Ordination (Zwölf Thesen)", in *Theologische Versuche*, II, ed. J. Rogge and G. Schille (Berlin, 1970), pp. 193–214.
[8] See, for example, the duplicated report on the "Bilateral Conversations of the World Confessional Confederations" submitted by N. Ehrenström and G. Gassmann to the Commission for Faith and Church Constitution at its meeting in August 1971 at Louvain.

possibility of recognition of each other's office is also referred to by the study commission "Gospel and Church". The reasons given for this possible recognition are the new understanding of apostolic succession, stressing the teaching of the apostles, a mutual recognition of abundant doctrinal apostolicity and increasing acceptance of the multiplicity of the New Testament offices. To this may be added the Lutheran conviction that the Gospel can also make use of the Catholic structure of office, so long as this is understood as a human and ecclesiastical right. This even applies to the Papacy as a visible sign of unity, excluding the special aspect of infallibility as defined by the First Vatican Council.[9]

II. CONSEQUENCES

Bearing in mind the present situation in the churches as outlined above, how are we to proceed *theologically* towards a recognition of each other's offices? There are, I believe, three questions above all which have to be discussed in this context, the ecclesiological problem, the problem of scripture and tradition and the problem of the Gospel and law.

(a) *The Ecclesiological Problem*

Is it possible for both Catholics and Lutherans to agree that the Church is essentially a group of people sent out into the world by the same Lord to proclaim the Gospel, just as Christ himself was sent into the world by the Father (John 20. 21; cf. 1 Peter 2. 9)? If the Church is understood as a "community of witness and service",[10] the question of particular offices would automatically become secondary compared with the conviction that all Christians have an apostolic office as those sent out by the Lord.

What would be the meaning of this in connection with the problem of apostolic succession? Is it not possible that the

---

[9] I cannot unfortunately go into the debate about the recent book on papal infallibility by H. Küng, *Unfehlbar?* (Zürich, Einsiedeln and Cologne, [2]1970).

[10] This is one of the formulae used by the united Evangelical churches of the German Democratic Republic to express their understanding of themselves as churches.

churches might perhaps come to realize that they have hitherto had too one-sided a view of each other as official hierarchies or pastoral offices?

(b) *The Problem of Scripture and Tradition*

What binding force does the structure of the churches, as these have developed in the course of history, have on what we do now in the Church? It would, I am convinced, be of enormous help in the movement towards a mutual recognition of office if both churches could agree that the only essential tradition is the biblical tradition and that it is only on the basis of this tradition that any decision can be made concerning how much binding force the traditional structures of the Church may have. The plurality of offices in the early Church, as delineated in the New Testament and in the different versions of the concept of the apostles,[11] would, I think, inevitably result in a new understanding. On the one hand, the homogeneous episcopal constitution of the Western Church, together with the primacy of the Pope in matters of jurisdiction, would not necessarily be abandoned. On the other hand, the function of the uninterrupted chain of laying on of hands would also continue to be regarded as valuable. Neither, however, would remain, in the light of the New Testament witness, the *conditio sine qua non* of being a church.

(c) *The Problem of the Gospel and Law*

Underlying the problem of office generally is the question whether Christ should be regarded as the legislator of the Church. Has canon 21 of the Tridentine Decree on Justification, which affirmed that Christ was this legislator, really been fully and exhaustively discussed? W. Steinmüller has provided an excellent review of the different attitudes taken in the Evangelical Church towards this question[12] and Catholic views of the matter are also very divergent. The task given by the Lord to the Church

---

[11] See, for example, the first appendix of the document on Catholicity and Apostolicity accepted by the joint working group of Roman Catholics and the Ecumenical Council and published in *Ökumenische Rundschau*, 20 (1971), pp. 105 ff.

[12] W. Steinmüller, *Evangelische Rechtstheologie*, I and II (Cologne and Graz, 1968).

to preach the Gospel and to celebrate the sacraments[13] undoubtedly confronts the Church with a legal question.

The question of human relationships under the law of Christ
can, however, only be understood correctly within the context
of God's promise and offer of grace and man's acceptance in
faith. It is essentially different from statutory laws which define
human relationships based on superiority and inferiority and
other limits of jurisdictional authority and give them an institutional character, laws which can ultimately be grouped under
the two headings of commandment and obedience.

Is it true to say that Christ was the legislator in his Church in
this "secular" sense? The *satis est* of article 7 of the *Confessio
Augustana* may, I think, throw a helpful and positive light on
this question. Also it is difficult in this context to distinguish
clearly between human law and the law of God.[14] Although the
norm that must be applied to this law is whether it serves the
task of preaching the Gospel, the law itself must be constantly
expressed in new forms adapted to changing historical circumstances.

In conclusion, I shall very briefly consider how we can *in
practice* come to a mutual recognition of office. I should like
simply to point to three possibilities. Firstly, the churches ought
to take to heart the findings and recommendations of the expert
bodies set up by them. Secondly, we should cease to try to create
a "super-Church" with a single, unified structure. We should
regard a plurality of structures within the one Church as a very
suitable possibility and give up all idea of a "return" on the part
of all separated churches to the one structure. Finally, we should
allow as much latitude as possible to pluriformity within the
existing confessional structure.

Translated by David Smith

---

[13] It is not possible to discuss here precisely how we ought to speak of an
institution of the sacraments by Christ.

[14] See the report mentioned in note 8 above; the commission "Gospel and
Church" discusses here whether it is still possible to make a sharp distinction between human law and the law of God in the Church.

3. A Methodist Reply

Albert Outler

THE EARLY stages of ecumenical dialogue are often subtly self-deceiving. The heart-lifting discovery that one or another of the ancient dividers of the churches can be overcome (at least in principle) by ampler analyses of the original issues[1] readily raises hopes for further progress that are then strangely and stubbornly deferred. Mutual recognition between separated Christians normally begins with their mutual confession of the Lordship of Christ and then moves in concentric spirals towards co-operation, on the one hand, and doctrinal consensus, on the other. Sooner or later, however, the dialogue begins to stagger as resistance to real change builds up and then even the ecumenical zealots have to come to terms with the tragic fact that separation persists and that at the centre of it all is the division of our eucharistic ministries. Here is where the burdens of our separate histories weigh down heaviest; here our loyalties to our diverse traditions remain as barriers to further progress.

Yet it has also been clear, from the very beginnings of modern ecumenism, that the formula of "reunion by return" (i.e., abjuration and re-ordination) is not a live option for "separated brethren", because one of our most crucial convictions is that our ministries, with all their faults, are still not wholly invalid and, therefore, it would be bad faith for us to say otherwise. These orders may, indeed, be "irregular", but they have been honoured in their exercise by the Holy Spirit and cannot be repudiated without dishonouring the Spirit. They were received in good faith and they have borne spiritual fruit, beyond all private charisms or personal merit. Here is the ecumenical crux —and it has been all along. Is there any way that schism and separation can be overcome without forfeiting the values of con-

[1] As, for example, in the now classic statement on "The Grace of our Lord Jesus Christ" (Edinburgh, 1937), or in Hans Küng's epochal study of *Justification* (1964), or in the *Dei Verbum* of Vatican II.

tinuity ("apostolic succession") or denying the validity of schismatic orders? Can apostolicity be interpreted in any other terms than the traditional claims of literal, unflawed episcopal succession? These are some of the baffling questions that have slowed the ecumenical parade from its earlier forward march to its present shuffling standstill.

I. The Methodist Point of View

For their part, Methodists have no theoretical difficulty with the principle of mutual recognition of presently divided ministries. Any person, baptized and confirmed in the Christian faith, is eligible for membership in any Methodist church. Similarly, any ordained minister in good standing in any other Christian church may apply for membership in a Methodist Annual Conference, subject only to the canonical requirements respecting his "Christian experience" and "professional competence". This comes with our Wesleyan heritage of "catholic spirit"—expressed in Wesley's famous dictum that, "as to all opinions [and practices] which *do not strike at the root of Christianity*, we [Methodists] think and let think".[2] This early tradition of ecumenical openness [*not* "indifferentism"] has often been reaffirmed.[3]

This means that, in practice, Methodists receive and demit members by letters of transfer without ecclesiological prejudice. Similarly, ordained ministers from other churches must satisfy the same general requirements set for all Methodist ordinands but with no question of re-ordination. Nor is there any objection, on principle, to dual or multiple ministerial affiliations. The Table of the Lord is open to all baptized Christians who can respond to the ritual "invitation" (borrowed from the Book of Common Prayer): "Ye that do truly and earnestly repent of your sins, etc. . . . draw near with faith, etc. . . . ." And as for co-operative ecumenical ventures—community festivals, picket lines, ecumenical celebrations, etc.—the only obstacles to Methodist

---

[2] "The Character of a Methodist" (*Works*, viii, pp. 339–47). See also, "Catholic Spirit" (*Works*, v, pp. 492–504).

[3] Cf. the "Resolution on the Cause of Christian Unity", in *The Book of Resolutions of the United Methodist Church* (1968).

participations are our plentiful human foibles but not our church law or policy.

Actually our dilemma is just the other way around. Already we have a working relation of mutual recognition with the ministries of other "free churches" (save those with "closed communions") and also with most of the churches in the Presbyterian and Reformed traditions. But with the Lutherans we (or they) have the still unsolved problem of "pure doctrine"; and with the Anglicans, Roman Catholics and Orthodox, we (or they) have the still unsolved problem of "the historic episcopate in apostolic succession". By Lutheran standards, our doctrines are too "catholic" (i.e., synergistic) and by Catholic standards, our presbyterial succession (for that is what it amounts to, despite bishops in the Methodist churches of American derivation) is irregular and schismatic.

Even so, Methodists have continued to affirm their allegiance to the Christian tradition[4] and to the vital core of catholic Christian teaching. This core—variously expressed—focuses in the catholic doctrine of the Triune God, in the mystery of man's salvation in and through Jesus Christ and in an evangelical ethic of "faith filled with the energy of love".[5] In their standards of doctrine, Methodists seek to honour the intent of the historic creeds and confessions, even as they welcome new developments in liturgy and theology. It is this attempted synthesis of "evangelical" and "catholic" that has been the hallmark of Methodism at its best. And at least occasionally others have noticed it—as in an important communication "from the Vatican" to the United Methodist Church:

This dialogue has brought us an understanding of the many Christian treasures which Methodists and Catholics share. At the heart of these there appears an intense conviction of the fullness of divine mercy, of the efficacy of Christ's saving work and of the reality of God's grace. Hence we share a high ambition of "scriptural holiness"—a personal, continuous and disciplined growth in conformity to Christ—which finds its

[4] Cf. "The Renewal of the Christian Tradition", Faith and Order Paper No. 40, in Faith and Order Findings (1963), pp. 7-27.
[5] Wesley's trans. of Galatians 5. 6 in "Catholic Spirit", op. cit., p. 497.

setting in the social reality of the Church committed to the Gospel for the service to the world.[6]

II. New Developments

But it is just this sort of mutual recognition—which comes also from the Anglicans and even from the Orthodox in a more limited sense—that is also the principal source of our ecumenical frustration, as far as our ministries are concerned. How does my Wesleyan (and therefore Anglican!) theology serve me ecumenically, as far as my ministerial office is concerned? How many Methodists, since Vatican II, have prayed the mass with their Roman brethren with real devotion—and have linked their hearts and arms in many good causes—and still find themselves fenced off from their holiest "common cause", except for occasional irregular eucharists that are not truly "representative", and therefore not truly catholic? I have preached the homily in a Catholic bishop's private chapel, and then not been offered communion—by one of my dearest friends. I have been offered communion by other Catholic friends—and have had to decline it, not on *my* principles, but *theirs!*

And yet it is just the irony and agony of these incomplete recognitions that may be the beginnings of a shift from traditional catholic notions of "regularity" to newer and thus far underdeveloped, notions of "validity" that may help to integrate the equal claims of *apostolicity* (historical continuity) and of *spiritual unity* ("the unity of the Spirit in the bond of peace" [Eph. 4. 3]). Increasingly, our common confession that "Jesus Christ *is* Lord and Saviour, to the glory of God the Father" (Phil. 2. 11) hacks away at our barriers without necessarily oversimplifying the doctrinal enterprise. Moreover, there is a deepening awareness that our mutually recognized baptisms already constitute the basic level of our *communicationes in sacris*—that they are something more than "clinical" or "lay" baptisms. Then, in a pragmatic sense, the fact that the divided churches have grown accustomed to each other *as churches* is beginning to produce *de facto* recognitions of various kinds. This has happened in the World

---

[6] Letter from Jean Cardinal Villot (Secretary of State) to the General Conference of the United Methodist Church (14 July 1971).

Council of Churches (despite the hedgings of their Toronto Declaration of 1950). And it was one of the crucial issues in the evolution of the text of *Unitatis Redintegratio* in the successive sessions of Vatican II. Now, how far does this mutual recognition of divided churches point us towards a more truly complete recognition of our several ministries?

One of the most interesting developments in this area—and for the Methodists especially—is the uncondemned thesis of some Catholics that at least some of the Protestant ministries might very well be redefined, not as schismatic or heretical, but rather as "extraordinary"—in the sense that their historical circumstances need to be taken into account in all reappraisals of their validity.[7]

This, *mutatis mutandis*, is very close to Wesley's understanding of his own leadership-role in the Methodist movement and of the movement itself. He lived and died as an ordained presbyter in good standing in the Church of England (*minister ordinarius*). But the circumstances of his ministry in his own time and place—and its fruits!—convinced him of a divine calling to an *extraordinary ministry*, within the church and for the church (*intentio faciendi quod facit ecclesia*). He drew the line between the "prophetic" ministry of laymen (preaching, Christian counsel and public witness) and the ordained ministry (the sacraments and church order). His societies were conceived of as church auxiliaries. The Methodists were taught to depend on the church for their sacraments, and Wesley consistently opposed all separatist impulses—even while he was in the swirl of a great revival that the establishment could not assimilate.[8]

He believed (and on *Anglican* authority, he thought) that nonepiscopal ordinations (e.g., Protestant ordinations on the Con-

---

[7] Cf. F. J. van Beeck, "Towards an Ecumenical Understanding of the Sacraments", in *The Journal of Ecumenical Studies*, 3, no. 1 (Winter, 1966), p. 90: "In view of the extraordinary situation, the *bona fides*, and the authenticity of the *diakonia*, supported by the faith and ecclesial character of their communities, the ministry of (the Word and) the sacraments as exercised by Protestant ministers may in terms of the Roman Catholic church order be qualified as *recognizable* as an extraordinary ministry." See also similar studies by J. Colson and D. O'Hanlon.

[8] Cf. Frank Baker, *John Wesley and the Church of England* (New York, 1970).

tinent) might be recognized as valid in principle. And he was further convinced that the historical claims of a literal, unflawed episcopal succession were unproved and unprovable—what with the penumbral zones in early church history, the presbyterial successions in Alexandria, the anomalies of papal history, the skewed records of Orthodoxy under the Turks, the tumults of the sixteenth century, etc. Thus, although he favoured episcopacy as optimal, he regarded the presbyterate as the most truly stable agency of the church's historical continuity. Thus, he understood himself, in his "extraordinary" ministerial mission as "a scriptural *episcopos*, as much as any man in England or in Europe".[9]

It was to this principle—that historical emergencies may legitimize historical irregularities—that he appealed in his decisive break with the Anglican hierarchy, and for the Methodist people in the U.S.A., not England. When it became clear to him, after the Revolution, that the American societies had no available sacramental ministry and no prospect for one, he undertook to provide them with an emergency ministry upon his own authority, again as *minister extraordinarius*—using the form of a hastily convoked "presbytery" of Anglican priests in Bristol (2 September 1784).[10]

That these ordinations were irregular (and therefore schismatic in Anglican terms) need not be denied—even if one disregards the ironic fact that Anglican orders stand in an analogous relationship to Rome. The crucial question is whether or not, given the actual alternatives in the actual historical circumstances, Anglicans and Romans are still compelled to judge that the Methodist ministry thus constituted is also invalid. If so, then re-ordination (or ordination!) would obviously be in order —and also quite out of the question. If not, then the ecumenical task is to find a formula that can allow for "regularization" without abjuration (whether express or implied). But if one has ever got to this point, one might also wonder how then Methodist orders differ from Anglican, *in principle*? If Rome can recognize Anglican orders without reformulating her traditional defini-

⁹ Letter to Charles Wesley, in the *Arminian Magazine*, 1786, pp. 50–1; cf. *Letters*, VII, 284.
¹⁰ Cf. Gerald F. Moede, *The Office of Bishop in Methodism* (Zürich, 1964), Ch. 1; see also Frank Baker, *op. cit.*, Ch. 15.

tions of schism, how many other Protestant churches might then be included in the same formula? *Why not* some "uniate" *Western* churches in communion with Rome?

Since 1784, Methodists have tended to understand the ministerial office chiefly in terms of mission and function. The notion is elliptical, with one focus on the ordinand's "inner call" and the other on the church's validation of each alleged vocation after a public examination of "gifts, graces and fruits". This is always the act of an Annual Conference (the Methodist equivalent of Lutheran synods or Reformed presbyteries) and is a necessary precondition for ordination. Thus while Methodist *polity* is "connectional" (i.e., dominated by its ecclesiastical officers), the Methodist ministerial *succession* is conciliar and collegial.

Our rituals for ordination are largely adaptations of the Anglican ordinal, with similar formal intentions. It goes without saying that the fruits of the ministries authorized by such ordinations and intentions have been sadly uneven and imperfect, and all too often (why deny it?) unfaithful. But we would quickly insist that *this* sort of invalidity is not a function of "irregularity". And yet it is our "irregularity", not our validity or invalidity, that has been the schismatic bone of contention between our churches. "Regularization"—which is to say, the overcoming of *schism*—is therefore a prime ecumenical goal. Can it be done on something resembling Father van Beeck's proposals—and if so, how could it be done, practically? And, in any case, what are the conceivable alternatives?

III. Two Concrete Proposals

Two proposals reflecting this idea of the mingling of mutually recognized (or recogniz*able*) ministries are currently in negotiation, in England and the U.S.A.—and both are currently stymied. In England, there is a plan for the reunion of the Church of England and the Methodist Church, with a common confession of faith and a proposed "service of reconciliation", in which mutual prayers and layings-on of hands would allow all parties involved to give and receive all the enduements of their respective traditions of ministry, under the impartial presidency of the Holy Spirit. Would this amount to covert re-ordination?

In the first crucial vote (1969), both churches produced majorities in favour of the plan, but the Church of England's tally fell short of the required two-thirds. Incidentally, one of the Anglican objections to the plan was that it might endanger the prospects of Rome's reversal of its traditional rejection of Anglican orders!

The Consultation on Church Union in the United States (in which four Methodist churches are involved, along with five other churches, including the Episcopal) has produced a tentative agreement that the ministries of the several member churches already recognize each other as valid and that, therefore, they can be reconciled and mingled without re-ordination. The proposed ritual for this service of reconciliation has two stages. Stage One envisages mutual acts of repentance, mutual acceptance and a new act of covenanting in a new ministry for the new church. Stage Two would then allow each of the ministries thus mingled to offer to the others all the spiritual gifts and apostolic authority that can thus be transmitted (the Kiss of Peace, prayers, the layings-on of hands, etc.). This, presumably, would bring all the ministries into episcopal and presbyterial parity—with all other conveyable graces! None of the ministries thus mingled would have forfeited its own distinctive heritage and all would have gained a greater fullness.

And yet the impasse to which both these plans have come is a sobering reminder of the tenacity of the tradition that schisms must be healed, if at all, by a return to the *status quo ante*. Loyalties to tradition and loyalties to the Spirit are snarled together and all of us are still harvesting the bitter fruits of schism.

But traditions function best only when history is unfolding smoothly, when the prospective future is enough like the remembered past so that both may be conceived symmetrically. And yet who supposes that ours is such a time or that any of our surviving traditions can cope with any of our conceivable future prospects—without recourse to some sort of truly "extraordinary" venture of imagination and healing love? Given the undiminished imperatives to Christian unity under which all the churches stand (condemned, one thinks, for their apathy and indifference) and given our recent but enlarging experiences of mutual recognition and mutual co-operation in ministry, can we hope and pray for yet another ecumenical breakthrough—in which the gap between the "ordinary" and "extraordinary" ministries thrown up by the tragic vicissitudes of our separate histories might be bridged, by divine grace and human magnanimity? Is it only an empty dream that the time draws on when Christians in every place who realize their *koinonia* in Christ may also enjoy that communion that rightfully belongs to every member of Christ's Body and thus become more truly valid witnesses to his life and death and victory?

4. *An Anglican Reply*

Massey Sheperd

THE Anglican Communion is a fellowship of some twenty self-governing, autonomous churches that share a common ethos of doctrine, worship and discipline, stemming from the Reformation of the sixteenth century when the Church of England severed its ties with the Roman See. The separation was due primarily to political circumstances, but was reinforced by significant theological, liturgical and juridical changes from the patterns of medieval Western Christendom.

Whatever the occasion and circumstances of the sixteenth-century Reformation, the Anglican churches have always claimed unbroken continuity in faith and order with the universal Church of antiquity—transmitted in dual streams from the ancient British-Irish foundations of late Roman imperial times, and from the mission sent by Pope Gregory the Great to the English people in the late sixth century. Anglicans accept the creeds and doctrinal decisions of the first seven ecumenical councils as legitimate interpretations of the scriptural revelation. Their liturgies, contained in the several recensions of the Book of Common Prayer, preserve the basic structures and substance of worship as developed in the Western Church. And they insist upon maintaining the threefold orders of bishop, priest (presbyter) and deacon in succession from apostolic and early Christian times.

The unity and collegiality of the Anglican churches are symbolized in the consultative Lambeth Conferences of all Anglican bishops, who have normally met since 1867 at ten-year intervals, by the invitation and under the presidency of the Archbishop of Canterbury. The reports and resolutions of these Conferences have no canonical authority; but they provide important agreements in doctrinal and practical concerns—especially in matters of church unity—which have persuasive influence upon the policies and continuing loyalties of the Anglican churches with one another.

Since the inception of the modern Ecumenical Movement at the World Missionary Conference in Edinburgh (1910), the Anglican Communion has actively participated in the struggle for Christian reunion. The Lambeth Conference of 1920 reaffirmed its quadrilateral platform for discussion and negotiation for unity in its well-known "Appeal to All Christian People":

The Holy Scriptures, as the record of God's revelation of himself to man, and as being the rule and ultimate standard of faith; and the creed commonly called Nicene, as the sufficient statement of the Christian faith, and either it or the Apostles' Creed as the baptismal confession of belief:

The divinely instituted sacraments of Baptism and the Holy Communion, as expressing for all the corporate life of the whole fellowship in and with Christ:

A ministry acknowledged by every part of the Church, as possessing not only the inward call of the Spirit, but also the commission of Christ and the authority of the whole body.

In regard to the last point, the ministry, the "Appeal" went on to reiterate the Anglican position "that the episcopate is the one means of providing such a ministry":

It is not that we call in question for a moment the spiritual reality of the ministries of those Communions which do not possess the episcopate. On the contrary we thankfully acknowledge that these ministries have been manifestly blessed and owned by the Holy Spirit as effective means of grace. But we submit that considerations alike of history and of present experience justify the claim which we make on behalf of the episcopate. Moreover, we would urge that it is now and will prove to be in the future the best instrument for maintaining the unity and continuity of the Church. But we greatly desire that the office of a bishop should be everywhere exercised in a representative and constitutional manner, and more truly express all that ought to be involved for the life of the Christian Family in the title of Father-in-God.

A first step in the implementation of the Lambeth "Appeal" came in 1931 with the agreement at Bonn between representatives of the Anglican and Old Catholic Churches, which established full intercommunion between these Churches; namely, that "each Communion recognizes the catholicity and independence of the other and maintains its own"; and that "intercommunion does not require from either Communion the acceptance of all doctrinal opinion, sacramental devotion, or liturgical practice characteristic of the other, but implies that each believes the other to hold all the essentials of the Christian Faith".

Out of this agreement with the Old Catholics, including the Polish National Catholic Church, has developed a new relationship of Anglicans to what is called The Wider Episcopal Fellowship: i.e., full intercommunion and recognition of ministries with churches that, from the Anglican standpoint, fulfil the Lambeth Quadrilateral, but do not intend to account themselves members of the Anglican Communion. At the same time, because of its autonomy, no single Anglican church is required without its own free consent to accept such agreements and concordats with non-Anglican and episcopal churches.

To date, agreements and concordats of Anglican churches have been made with a number of episcopal churches other than the Old Catholics, such as the Lutheran churches of episcopal polity in Sweden and Finland. In some cases, the mutual recognition of ministries has resulted from the "gift" of the episcopate in historical succession by Anglican churches themselves —to the Lusitanian Church, Catholic Apostolic, Evangelical (of Portugal), the Spanish Reformed Episcopal Church and the Philippine Independent Church.

The formation of the Church of South India in 1948, in which four Anglican dioceses participated, created a new problem. Unification and mutual recognition of ministry were achieved in the order of bishops, but not in the orders of priests and deacons. Hence the Anglican churches have delayed concordats of full, rather than partial, intercommunion until such time as the entire ministry of the Church of South India received episcopal ordination.

A more fruitful approach was made in 1970 to the union of Anglican and non-episcopal Protestant churches in North India and Pakistan—and (possibly) in Ceylon. Special rites for the unification of ministries were devised at the time of union, so that all orders of ministry may be accepted on the terms laid down in the Lambeth "Appeal" of 1920: "possessing not only the inward call of the Spirit, but also the commission of Christ and the authority of the whole body". It is along these lines that negotiations for unity between Anglicans and Protestants are proceeding in England, Canada, the United States, Nigeria and other places.

The peculiar stance of the Anglican Communion in matters of Christian reunion lies in its intransigent insistence upon maintaining the threefold orders of ministry and the "apostolic succession" of the episcopate. This succession was carefully guarded in the convolutions of the Reformation period, but without a precise theological consensus as to its meaning. Hence there was from the beginning an ambiguity within Anglicanism as to whether episcopacy was essential or only pragmatically beneficial to a truly Catholic Church.

This ambiguity has been reinforced by the efforts of Anglican theologians and apologists to defend episcopacy on historical and rational grounds, without positive proof that it belongs to the deposit of faith revealed in Scripture—hence the paradoxical situation in which Anglicanism finds itself in relation to ministries of other churches. (1) It accepts without question the validity of the ministry of the Roman Catholic Church, but finds its own ministry declared "null and void" on doctrinal grounds in Pope Leo XIII's *Apostolicae Curae* (1896). (2) The validity of Anglican orders has been favourably acknowledged by many of the Eastern Orthodox churches, but without further progress in steps leading to intercommunion. (3) Non-episcopal churches of Protestant conviction have spurned the Anglican *sine qua non* position on episcopacy as a negative judgment on their own ministries of word and sacrament, although in all official statements Anglicans have been careful not to make any such judgment on their ministries as real means of grace.

The Decree on Ecumenism of Vatican II opened a new era in the relationship of Roman Catholicism and Anglicanism, in its statement that among the Communions separated from the Roman See "the Anglican Communion occupies a special place" in the continuance of "some Catholic traditions and institutions" (ch. III, sec. 13). Following the official visit of the Archbishop of Canterbury to Pope Paul VI in March 1966, a Joint Preparatory Commission of the two Communions was appointed to explore the areas of difference that are crucial for any reconciliation of the schism of the sixteenth century. Consequent to its report (Malta, 2 January 1968), a permanent Theological Commission has been established, which is making progress in resolving issues concerning the doctrine of the Church, the sacraments and the ministry.

At the present time there is considerable optimism that the restoration of intercommunion is imminent in the not too distant future. Already in many local areas this is taking place *de facto*, though not *de iure*, and the pressures of this fact add considerable weight to the urgency of negotiation as well as to dialogue at official levels. In any case, there is a desire not to re-open what Pope John called "old quarrels", but to seek a common mind about what the ministry must and should mean and how it is to be exercised now and in the future.

The ultimate goal is the reintegration of the two Communions and their ministries. Its realization, however, is not at the moment foreseeable. Given the possible resolution of doctrinal differences (such as, from the Anglican standpoint, papal infallibility and the Mariological definitions) there remains a deep cleavage in juridical principles and procedures. It is most unlikely, for example, that the Anglican churches would abandon the participation of their laity at all levels of decision-making processes, or the non-veto of a primate over collegial decisions of the episcopate. Anglicans could accept the Pope as servant of the unity of the Church and its universal primate, but not the statement of *Lumen Gentium* (ch. III, sec. 22) that "the Roman Pontiff has full, supreme and universal power over the Church".

Two pragmatic proposals may be possible and viable in the more immediate future. One would unite the Anglican churches to the Roman See in a manner comparable to the Eastern Uniate churches. The difficulty for Anglicans in this proposal remains juridical, particularly as regards the "power" of the Pope. The other—more congenial to Anglicans, but perhaps less so to Roman Catholics—would be a relationship to the Roman Catholic Church such as the Anglican Communion enjoys with the Old Catholics and other churches of "The Wider Episcopal Fellowship". It is this solution that seems to be implicit in the Malta Report of the Joint Preparatory Commission:

> We recommend that the second stage in our growing together begin with an official and explicit affirmation of mutual recognition from the highest authorities of each Communion. It would acknowledge that both Communions are at one in the faith that the Church is founded upon the revelation of God the Father, made known to us in the person and work of Jesus Christ, who is present through the Holy Spirit in the Scriptures and his Church, and is the only mediator between God and Man, the ultimate authority for all our doctrine. Each accepts the basic truths set forth in the ecumenical creeds and the common tradition of the ancient Church, although neither Communion is tied to a positive acceptance of all the beliefs and devotional practices of the other.

Bibliography:

The Six Lambeth Conferences 1867–1920. Compiled under the Direction of the Most Reverend Lord Davidson of Lambeth (London, 1920). Resolutions and Reports of later Lambeth Conferences of 1930, 1948, 1958 and 1968 have been published separately.

Intercommunion Today, being the Report of the Archbishops' Commission on Intercommunion (London, 1968).

John Jay Hughes, *Absolutely Null and Utterly Void*, The Papal Condemnation of Anglican Orders, 1896 (Washington & London, 1968).

James B. Simpson and Edward M. Story, *The Long Shadows of Lambeth X*, A Critical Eye-Witness Account of the Tenth Decennial Conference of 462 Bishops of the Anglican Communion (New York, 1969).

William H. Van de Pol, *Anglicanism in Ecumenical Perspective* (Duquesne Studies, Theological Series, 4) (Pittsburgh, 1965).

5. A Free Church Reply

Franklin Littell

THE characteristics of the Free Church point of view have been developed earlier in *Concilium* by the present writer.[1] With this in mind, it is only necessary here to emphasize those points related to the main question: "How can we bring about, theologically and practically, a mutual recognition of the ministries?"

The Free Church position was first concretely manifest in the sixteenth-century *Taüfer*, who held a view of the Church and church history which is technically called "primitivism". They made normative use of their vision of the early Church ("cultural primitivism") and they regarded the period of the house churches of the *Acts of the Apostles* as the golden age of Christianity ("chronological primitivism").[2] They contradicted the traditional understanding, which since Augustine and Orosius dated the final earthly period of church history from the founding of the Church. They claimed a "fall of the Church" had occurred with Constantine's establishment of the Christian religion as the official cult of the Roman Empire, and they asserted their own movement(s) to be the "restitution" or "restoration" of the primitive (and normative) model.

[1] F. H. Littell, "The Concerns of the Free Churches", *Concilium*, 4, 2 (1966), pp. 46–9; U.S. edn., Vol. 14.
[2] The concept of "primitivism" and its significance for Free Church understandings is elaborated in F. H. Littell and H. H. Walz (eds.), *Weltkirchenlexikon* (Stuttgart, 1960), 1182–7.

The threefold scheme of golden age, fall and restitution runs throughout the "Radical Reformation", and it creates a fault-line of geological proportions between the "magisterial Reformation"[3] and the Free Church type. To the latter belong all of those churches which are descended from restitution(s) which took place in the Left Wing of the Reformation, in radical Puritanism, in Pietism and the Evangelical Awakening, and during the nineteenth-century revivals in North America. (To the latter also belong numerous heterodox movements such as the Church of Latterday Saints—commonly called "Mormons", the Church of Christ, Scientist, and Jehovah's Witnesses.)

In the contemporary scene, a special kind of thoroughgoing Christian primitivism—Pentecostalism—has become important to churchmen and theologians. Whereas Bible-centred groups such as the sixteenth-century Anabaptists in Europe and the nineteenth-century "Restoration Movement" in the U.S.A. (called "Christians" or "Disciples") attempted in literal fashion to reconstitute the ministries they read from the New Testament, the Pentecostal movement takes a more clearly anti-institutional and anti-structural path. For the Pentecostals, the Early Church was the period before formalized theology and structured authority arose in Christendom: the whole Church was then called to prophesy, to manifest the gifts of the Spirit, to exercise the power of charismatic faith. For the Pentecostals, the time of restitution is marked by new manifesations of the mighty works of God through an inspired and missionary church. On many mission fields—particularly in Central America, West Africa, and among the blacks of the West Indies and the U.S.A.—the Pentecostal movement (e.g., the Church of the Four Square Gospel, the Assemblies of God, the Church of God in Jesus Christ) has lately attracted considerable attention from missiologists and ecumenists. The movement is sometimes referred to as a "Third Force" on the world map of Christianity.

The Style of the Restitution(s)

In the sixteenth century there were already two sectors of restitutionist Protestantism of importance to our theme, the

[3] G. H. Williams, *The Radical Reformation* (Philadelphia, 1962) pp. xxiii–vi.

Biblicists (*Taüfer*) and those who emphasized especially the un-structured work of the Spirit (*Spiritualisten*).[4] Of the latter style, only the Schwenckfelder Church with 6,000 members (chiefly in Pennsylvania) remains as a memorial to the work and memory of a sixteenth-century leader. Of the Bible-centred, the Mennon-ites are the most important in the direct line. In spite of the difference in emphasis, over four and a half centuries those Free Churches stressing first the return of the power of the Spirit have always settled sooner or later into clear ecclesiological and litur-gical patterns. And those tending to reconstitute literally the New Testament ordinances have usually—with a few rare ex-ceptions like the Quaker theologian Robert Barclay—preferred to speak of the divine initiative in human history in the language of the Third Person rather than the Second Person of the Holy Trinity.[5]

The churches of the Restitution conceived of the True Church (*die reine Kirche*, a phrase used deliberately to contrast with the centrality of *die reine Lehre* in Lutheranism) as an eschatological community, a pilgrim people "cut loose from the world". They utterly repudiated the whole idea of *corpus christianum*, treat-ing Christendom as missionary territory in the same sense as Africa, India or China. The Call, to which only adults who have reached the "age of understanding" can adequately respond, came by the witness of the word and service. The Great Com-mission (Mt. 28. 18–20, Mk. 16. 15–16) was a favourite proof-text. Enlightenment, faith, conversion and rebirth were followed by the "sealing" of the Elect by baptism. By this act each Chris-tian was ordained into the ministry of the whole people, whose Head was Jesus Christ. As special gifts of the Spirit were evident in some members, they were singled out as apostles, prophets and teachers—all of them charismatic functions (1 Cor. 12. 28). Above all, the calling was authenticated by practical service. To be an apostle was to be a servant, to share in the diaconate. The

---

[4] Alfred Hegler first developed this important distinction between types of restitutionists in his classic, *Geist und Schrift bei Sebastian Franck* (Frei-burg, 1892), and his lead was followed by Ernst Troeltsch and others.

[5] F. H. Littell, "Some Free Church Remarks on the Concept, the Body of Christ", in R. S. Pelton (ed.), *The Church as the Body of Christ* (Notre Dame, 1963), pp. 127-38.

ministry was a collective one, within which certain were chosen for representative offices.

The whole people shared the ministry, which was validated as an extension of Christ's ministry. This ministry of the whole authenticated the special offices, which had no existence apart from it. The whole people possessed the "Key of David" (to unlock Scripture) and the "Key of Peter" (to loose and to bind in this life and eternally). Among the sixteenth-century Hutterites the only special offices recognized were those of the *Diener des Wortes* and *Diener der Notdurft*, terms whose NT equivalents will readily spring to the reader's mind. Among the seventeenth-century Quakers both the form of sound words and the programme of action were fixed by "the sense of the meeting". The authority of the Spirit, expressed in some earlier Christian generations by the whole Church in council, was located by the radical Protestants in the local congregation (initially house churches where two or three were gathered together). The basic principle of church government was the *consensus fidelium*, and they asserted this could only be determined where the whole people participated in the decision-making process. In some groups this led eventually to the sending of "travelling friends" between congregations, in others to the constitution of delegated assemblies; the experience of face-to-face encounter in the local congregation remained, however, primary.

Early Free Church men rejected all state-church structures, including rule by either hierarchy or civil government in matters of faith. Under toleration and—later—religious liberty, some Free Churches modified the points of commitment to a disciplined counter-culture—abandoning non-resistance or adult baptism or simple dress or church discipline or some other testimony. But before such accommodation set in, with prosperity and statistical success, all restitutionists practised a vigorous imitation of what they understood to be the style and mood of Christian life in the apostolic age. At the centre of this was a group ministry, a ministry of the whole believing people.

The Encounter with Catholicism

For the founders of Free Churches—men like Menno Simons, Robert Browne, George Fox, Alexander Mack, John Wesley,

Alexander Campbell—both Catholicism and the Protestant establishments belonged to the "fallen" period of the Church. They suffered persecution at the hands of both, and that persecution itself proved to them that the established churches were false (*vermeinten Christen*) and that they themselves were re-living the experience of the early Church.

Since the early Church settled both doctrinal and practical matters by reference to the Spirit in the meeting, the Free Churches were as suspicious of the science of Theology as they were of the science of administering a sophisticated and elaborate church law. Many of them are to this day as suspicious of theologians and church lawyers as they were of "the world". Here again is evidence of the primitivist orientation, of the built-in hostility to *Techne*.[6] The most conservative among them, like the Amish in the U.S.A., are frequently accused of opposition to education. But this is false: they are opposed to education which serves scientific objectives, the objectives of a civilization which they believe to have been committed for more than four centuries to war and violence and the coercion of human souls. They are strongly in favour of "education for life", by which they mean education in fitness for Christian life now and for the life to come. But it becomes difficult, of course, for men who are products of the universities to develop effective dialogue with men who believe that Christians should cultivate the simple life and seek their guidance from the Spirit in the church meeting.

The Free Church rejection of all church offices not specifically named in the New Testament and of all church structures which have grown up out of accommodation to civil government makes dialogue between them and the Catholic, Orthodox and Protestant churches which still maintain the vision of "Christendom" very precarious. The cornerstone of their witness lies in rejection of "the Constantinian settlement" and normative use of the model of the early Church, a model they believe to be commanded by both Scripture and Spirit. Even churches of that tradition which have prospered so mightily that they have become social establishments, if not legal, still have covert views of

[6] F. H. Littell, "Sectarian Protestantism and the Pursuit of Wisdom", in D. A. Erickson (ed.), *Public Controls for Non-Public Schools* (Chicago, 1969), pp. 61–82.

the True Church and the proper periodization of church history which explode in the midst of ecumenical dialogue—to the astonishment of all participants, including those who suddenly rediscover their own hidden presuppositions.

Nevertheless, there are changes in the general scene which tend to break down the Free Churches' total rejection of fellowship with the formerly privileged state-churches. Perhaps the most obvious change has been a result of the encounter of the established churches of Europe with Communist and Fascist totalitarianism. If this encounter has produced wholesale apostasy among the baptized, it has made many aware that small Christian movements formerly despised as "heretics" or "sectarians" are by no means the most dangerous enemies of the faith in today's world. The coming of the World Council of Churches and the events in and surrounding Vatican II certainly owed much to the *KZ-Gemeinschaft*, and to the soul-searching of faithful churchmen during the tragedy of mass apostasy and the martyrdom of confessors like Metzger and Bonhoeffer.

Although some important churches of the Free Church line—notably the Southern Baptist Convention and the Old Mennonites—still refuse public fellowship with territorial churches in the Ecumene, a general openness to dialogue and co-operation is evident. The Pentecostals of Chile and Switzerland have joined the WCC, and a distinguished scholar of that movement—Dr Walter Hollenweger—served for several years as Director of the Department on Evangelism. An opening towards Catholicism is more problematic, because of the long-standing opposition to any hierarchies and any ministerial orders except the ministry of the whole people. (The fact that most Free Churches have developed their own hierarchies[7] commonly goes unrecognized within the ranks.)

Specific Points of Contact

In the work of Vatican II several strategic lines have been opened for communication with the Free Churches. *Dignitatis*

[7] The very wise discussion of this matter by the Episcopalian Walter Lowrie, with his suggestions on its implications for mutual recognition of orders, has not yet received the attention it deserves; cf. *Ministers of Christ*, ed. T. O. Wedel (New York, 1964), Ch. III.

Humanae, with its affirmation of the right of the human person to religious freedom immune from coercion by any human power, has enormous practical importance. Chap. V of *Lumen Gentium*, on the call of the whole Church to holiness, and Chap. VII, on the eschatological nature of the pilgrim Church, are formulations which meet the Free Church ecclesiology squarely. Other sections might be mentioned, especially those having to do with the service of the Church to the needs of human persons in the world (*Gaudium et Spes*). When to these are added such compassionate concerns as presented in *Pacem in Terris*, *Mater et Magistra* and *Populorum Progressio*, the potential lines of communication and co-operation become many.

For there is a notable and historic openness of the Free Churches, in spite of their doctrine of separation, to consultation and co-operation where Christian service or mission is involved. On the other hand, many of them will not even send delegates to talk about institutional questions with sister churches of the same doctrine and polity. Here too the line of attack must be quite different from that which can be made with churches of clear structures and established lines of authority. Episcopalians and Lutherans and Presbyterians, for example, can send church diplomats with clear instructions, enabled from history and church law to define points of institutional agreement and disagreement. Baptists and Disciples and Pentecostals, for example, cannot; not primarily because they have a congregational form of government, but because they either traditionally consider the institutional forms fixed in their New Testament simplicity or relatively unimportant to spend time on (or both). What is important is the ministry of Christ's people, and all else is a function of that concern.

This bias does not reflect, as sometimes charged, a superficial "American" impatience for pragmatic action: it derives from a fundamental conviction as to what is really central to Christian faith and life.

What this means, concretely, is that the ecumenical consultations will draw more enthusiastic Free Church participation when they are centred not upon organizational questions but upon critical issues of Christian conscience and witness: e.g., the peace testimony, the encounter with totalitarian and post-Christian ideologies, racial injustice, the fight against colonial exploitation, the redemption of the city, and the like. When openness and mutual trust have been re-established on what they consider the heart of the Christian faith, they will be better able to accept the institutional changes which are necessary for a more charitable mutual recognition of the different offices of ministry.

6. A Catholic Reply
Maurice Villain

I SHALL restrict myself here to examination of a possible way to eucharistic reconciliation between Catholics and Protestants in a strictly limited context.

It goes without saying that the solution cannot come from *above*, from our respective authorities, who judge without leading the way forward, but must come from *below*, from small groups whose members are free to carry on their research and constantly present the results of their work to their churches in the hope of being given the green light.

I. PRESUPPOSITIONS

What follows is a working hypothesis, the result of many years of research in the Les Dombes group in France. This group, made up of about forty theologians (half of them Catholics and half Protestants, the Protestants being almost all from the Reformed tradition, though there are some Lutherans), has gradually achieved an important measure of agreement on anthropology, Christology, pneumatology and eschatology—this is a fundamental point to note. Our Protestant friends are now convinced that they belong with us to the same Western Church which was divided by the sixteenth-century Reformation—however serious this break may be, it is no more than incidental. This remark, fundamental to our case, is justified today by the best historians of the Reformation.[1] In other words, the Catholic Church is wounded. Since Vatican II it has given up the attempt to identify itself *simpliciter* with the Church of Jesus Christ; no doubt, as the Council declared,[2] it has preserved the principles of that Church in their fullness, but it has not preserved its image, and it will only recover this in communion with the other churches and ecclesial communities—this is the immense task of ecumenism.

But if this is true, the Catholic Church's Eucharist itself is injured. As a Catholic priest, I celebrate the Eucharist each day to nourish the faithful, and yet my deepest conviction makes me include a special prayer for pardon. Strictly, I should not presume to approach the holy mysteries when my separated Christian brothers are excluded, since they, too, have a rightful part in them, and I am deeply aware that the *confiteor* I say before the Eucharist with my community should mention this painful point. We Catholics do not "own" the Eucharist; Catholics and Protestants *together* have a duty to heal the injured Eucharist. We do not need to find out who has more and who has less; the first duty for all of us is to repent. The Les Dombes group is right to emphasize the need to spread a sense of "ecclesial *metanoia*" among Christian people—whose co-operation, in this way at least, is essential—and it is a source of grief to us that our people as a whole, for lack of mediators, is still far from this attitude.[3]

An interdenominational group which wants to solve the problem of reciprocal recognition of ministries must possess sufficient unity of faith, not merely on the important tenets of the Nicene creed, but specifically on eucharistic doctrine. In fact, on this point the Christian denominations show notable differences of interpretation. Without underestimating the striking complementarities

[1] On the Catholic side: J. Lortz, *La Réforme de Luther* (Paris, 1970–71); A. Ganoczy, *Calvin théologien de l'Eglise et du ministère* (Paris, 1964) and *Calvin et Vatican II, l'Eglise servante* (Paris, 1968).

[2] Decree *Unitatis Redintegratio*, 3.

[3] I am happy to be able to emphasize that things are quite different whenever a community is initiated into spiritual ecumenism (prayer and suffering for Christian unity).

here and there, we discover in general regrettable errors. Since this requirement of unity is in our view indispensable, it is worth dwelling on for a few moments.

How should we go about working out a doctrinal agreement? We decided that the best way was to start from the consensus reached at the 1967 Bristol conference and presented to the 1968 Uppsala assembly, because the resulting text, the fruit of an elaboration going back to the conferences in Lund and Montreal in 1952 and 1963, was approved at Uppsala by experts belonging to all the major churches, including official Roman Catholic representatives of the Unity Secretariat.[4]

Our group therefore decided to make a very careful study of this official text, then to clarify, recast and expand it on points which still create difficulty among us. At the date of writing (11 September) this work is complete, and we have an excellent text which was adopted unanimously. Since the complete text is too long to reproduce, I give a summary below.

The numbering of paragraphs will be seen to follow the general structure of the Bristol-Uppsala document mentioned in note 4:

1. The Eucharist, the Lord's meal; 2. The Eucharist, thanksgiving to the Father; 3. The Eucharist, a memorial of Christ; 4. The Eucharist, the gift of the Spirit; 5. The sacramental presence of Christ; 6. The Eucharist, a communion in the body of Christ; 7. The Eucharist, mission in the world; 8. The Eucharist, the banquet of the kingdom; 9. The president of the Eucharist; 10. Conclusion.

If the above list is compared with the contents list of the Bristol document, it will be seen that points 5, 8 and 9 of our text have been added to remove classical ambiguities, while point 7 of the Bristol document has been dropped. As an example of the approach to some delicate points we reproduce paragraphs 5 and 9 and part of the conclusion.

---

[4] See this text in *Verbum Caro* 87: "Accord œcuménique sur l'eucharistie", pp. 1–10. The structure is as follows: *Introduction and preamble; 1. The Eucharist, the Lord's meal; 2. The Eucharist, thanksgiving to the Father; 3. The Eucharist, a memorial (anamnesis) of Christ; 4. The Eucharist, a gift of the Spirit; 5. The Eucharist, a communion in the body of Christ; 6. The Eucharist, a mission in the world; 7. The Eucharist, an end of divisions.*

"The sacramental presence of Christ

"The eucharistic action is a gift of the person of Christ. The Lord said, 'Take and eat, for this is my body which is given up for you.' 'Drink of it, all of you; for this is my blood, the blood of the covenant, poured out for many for the remission of sins.' We therefore unanimously acknowledge the real, living and active presence of Christ in this sacrament.

"Discerning the body and blood of Christ requires faith. Nevertheless the presence of Christ to his Church in the Eucharist does not depend on the faith of the individual, because it is Christ who binds himself, by his words and in the Spirit, to the sacramental event, the sign of the gift of his presence.

"Since the act of Christ is the giving of his body and blood, that is, of himself, the reality given under the signs of bread and wine in his body and blood. (This does not mean either the physical presence of Christ in the bread and wine or a physico-chemical change in them. Cf. St Thomas, *S.T.* III 76, 3–5, and III 77, 3–8; Calvin, *Institutes* I, 11.13 and IV, 14.18.) It is in virtue of the creative word of Christ and through the power of the Holy Spirit that the bread and wine are made a sacrament and thus 'a participation in the body and blood' of Christ (1 Cor. 10.16). From that point they are, in their ultimate truth, under the outward sign, the reality given, and remain so in order to be eaten. What is given as the body and blood of Christ remains given as the body and blood of Christ and demands to be treated as such.

"Noting the diversity of practice among the churches (some Eastern churches—the Copts, for example—do not reserve the Eucharist), but relying on the agreement already reached and in order to bring about the ecclesial conversion (*metanoia*) agreed to be necessary (1969 and 1970 theses), we ask: that on the Catholic side it should be emphasized, especially in catechesis and preaching, that the main reason for reserving the Eucharist is to distribute it to the sick and the absent (*Eucharisticum mysterium*, 25 May 1967, Nos. 49, 50); that on the Protestant side efforts should be made to find the best way of showing proper respect to the elements which have been used in the eucharistic celebration (that is, their later consumption, without excluding their use for the communion of the sick).

"The president of the Eucharist

"In the Eucharist, Christ gathers and feeds his Church by inviting it to the meal at which he presides.

"The sign of this presiding function of Christ is the presiding function of a minister called and sent by him. The mission of ministers has its origin and norm in the mission of the apostles; it is transmitted in the Church by the imposition of hands with the invocation of the Holy Spirit. This transmission implies continuity of ministerial responsibility, fidelity to the apostolic teaching and a life modelled on the Gospel.

"The minister is a sign that the assembly does not own the act it is performing, that the Eucharist is not simply in its power, because it receives it from another, from Christ living in his Church. While remaining a member of the assembly, the minister is also that envoy who represents God's initiative and the link between the local community and the other communities in the universal Church.

"Through their mutual relations, the eucharistic assembly and its president live in dependence on the only Lord and High Priest. In its relation to the minister the assembly exercises its royal priesthood as a gift of Christ the priest. In his relation to the assembly, the minister in his presiding role lives in the service of Christ the shepherd."

In *Conclusion*, we recognized that "clarifications are still required with regard to the permanence of the sacramental presence and the precise form of the apostolic succession in the ministry. We feel that any common participation in the Eucharist demands a real effort to overcome these difficulties and eventually, on both sides, the abandonment of everything in denominational positions which is marked by polemic.

"The continuation of our work should further enrich the complementary spiritual values by which we live. We shall never exhaust our efforts to understand a mystery which is beyond all understanding and which invites us constantly to go out of ourselves to live in gratitude and wonder before this supreme gift of Christ to his Church."

I felt it necessary to insist on these presuppositions to ensure that the reader was aware of the requirements influencing the solution I now put forward.[5]

II. In Search of a Solution

Since this is a Catholic reply, I can do no better than take Vatican II as my basis. It is true that the *Decree on Ecumenism* does not say anything explicit about our problem, but it does contain a phrase which can form the basis of our reflections.[6] It is also true that our Protestant brothers are less than satisfied with the *Decree*; they feel they have been offered the bare minimum, and indeed it would have been possible to find a different formulation. On the Eucharist we read in the *Decree*: "especially because of a deficiency in the sacrament of orders (praesertim propter Sacramenti Ordinis defectum[7]) (the non-Roman ecclesial communities) have not preserved the genuine and total substance of the eucharistic mystery (genuinam atque integram substantiam Mysterii eucharistici non servasse)."

We may explain, on the authority of Cardinal Bea, that the word *substantia* was substituted by the Vatican Latinist for the *realitas* of the original text because *realitas* is not good Latin, but the word "substance" is liable to misunderstanding. We should translate: "The communities which stem from the Reformation *have not preserved the full reality of the eucharistic mystery*." What have they preserved, then? This is a question for theologians, and brings us to the heart of the problem.

We no longer have the right to reply, as in the past, with a verdict of invalidity, a purely legal reply which ignores the theologically positive elements which have been preserved. We must reply in terms of ecclesial character, because the *Decree* also attributes a real (though deficient) ecclesial character to the

[5] In parentheses I may add that in our view access to the Catholic Eucharist should not be denied, on grounds of belief about the Eucharist, to Christians of another denomination who adopt the substance of the faith professed in the Les Dombes outline.

[6] *Unitatis Redintegratio* III, 22.

[7] I have deliberately translated *defectus* by "deficiency" and not "absence", and this will be justified later. Cf. Abbott and Gallagher (eds), *The Documents of Vatican II* (London & New York, 1966), p. 364, which translates *defectus* by "lack" and *substantia* by "reality".

Protestant churches. They possess authentic elements of the eucharistic mystery, and this must include a form of ministry. Max Thurian, a sensitive interpreter of the *Decree*, rightly says that for the dialectic of *all* and *nothing* Vatican II has substituted the dialectic of *all* and *less*.[8] It is this *less*, this deficiency—or rather the positive element which remains—which we have to assess.

Given the presuppositions regarding the doctrine of the Eucharist mentioned in the first section, which were unanimously accepted by our group, the deficiency which has to be filled must relate strictly to the "ministry".

It is on this point that we as Catholics have the most serious difficulties in recognizing the ministry of our Reformed brothers, and these difficulties traditionally fall under three heads: the *priestly character, sacramental ordination* and the *apostolic succession*. These are traditional criteria; they were insisted on by the undivided Church before 1054 and the Eastern churches still require them in the same way as the Roman Catholic Church. The Faith and Order Commission, too, whose most recent conclusions we took as a starting-point, regards them as central, though it has not been able to offer an adequate solution.

It is our opinion that this threefold problem, exaggerated, distorted and taken to extremes in four centuries of polemics, is now beginning to be reintegrated into the main body of theology as a result of the work of ecumenical theology. We can bear witness to this from the steady evolution of our group in Les Dombes. I suggested some lines of research in this area in *Concilium*,[9] and other Catholic theologians have worked on these and take them further.[10] I shall now outline the position today.

---

[8] M. Thurian, "L'intercommunion fruit d'une foi commune", in *Vers L'Intercommunion* (Paris, 1970), pp. 45–48. I am greatly indebted to this lucid and courageous study.

[9] M. Villain, "Can there be Apostolic Succession outside the Continuity of the laying on of hands?" *Concilium*, April 1968, pp. 45–53 (U.S. edn., Vol. 34).

[10] B. Sesboüé, s.j., *Petite revue de presse théologique sur certains aspects du rapport: Esprit Saint, Eglise et ministère*. In this (duplicated) dossier prepared for the 1969 Les Dombes meeting our friend mentions: F.-X. Durrwell, *Lumen Vitae* (1969/1); G. Tavard, *Informations Catholiques Internationales* (15 July 1968); M. Leblanc, *Parole et Pain*, 30; W. Kasper, *Concilium*, March 1969 (U.S. edn., Vol. 43); P. Lebeau, *Nouvelle Revue*

1. *The Priestly Character of the Ministry*

Vatican II has given new emphasis to the ecclesial priesthood of the baptized in extremely strong terms (*Lumen Gentium*, 10–13; *Apostolicam Actuositatem*, 3 and 4), to such an extent, in fact, that if one today approaches the subject of the ministerial priesthood of the ordained, its shape emerges out of the priesthood of the baptized. But what is it? Certainly not a "doublet" of the one priesthood of Christ, as Protestants traditionally accused us of saying—and it must be admitted that our way of presenting the mass in teaching as a "repetition" of the sacrifice of the cross gave them some justification. It is only a particular form of participation in the one priesthood, to be precise, a sign, a specific sacramental reflection of Christ the head in the minister of the word and Eucharist, for the service of the priestly people.

If we re-read Calvin with irenical eyes, looking only for constructive values, we find, not indeed the word, always attacked as non-biblical, but certainly a reality close to it in content. I know devout disciples of the reformer who would subscribe to the following statement: "Within the ecclesial priesthood the Holy Spirit chooses for himself *ministers* who are fitted by ordination for the pastoral ministry (word and sacraments) through special gifts." This statement, in which the word "minister" has been substituted for the word "priest", in my opinion expresses a ministerial priesthood, and the minister who expressed himself in those words certainly believes that he has received a *permanent* vocation to the service of the word, the sacraments and unity. He has a sense of being a "convener", an "ambassador" accredited to his ministry, and no longer a layman. The whole argument of Max Thurian's penetrating book, *Sacerdoce et ministère*,[11] points towards an identity between the concepts of "minister" and "priest" and invites us Catholics to reassess the situation of our brother ministers as "priestly".

Théologique (January 1969); H. Fiolet, *Concilium*, April 1969 (U.S. edn., Vol. 44). To these may be added J. Moinget, "Intercommunion", *Etudes* (February 1970 and May 1971) and A. Hastings, "Intercommunion", *One in Christ* (1971/1).

[11] M. Thurian, *Sacerdoce ea ministère, recherche oecuménique* (Taizé, 1970).

2. Sacramental Ordination

Can the ordination of a minister of the Reformed Church be described as "sacramental"? This point was discussed in the article in *Concilium* already mentioned (n. 9). Personally, I owe much to the study by Leopold Schummer, *Le ministère pastoral dans l'Institution chrétienne de Calvin à la lumière du 3e sacrement* (Wiesbaden, 1965). Calvin regarded pastoral ordination as equivalent to a sacrament which conferred special gifts of the Spirit for the exercise of ministries.[12] Max Thurian is as clear as one could wish on this point in his exegesis of the reformer,[13] as is A. Ganoczy (a Catholic) in his conclusions on "common ground between Calvinist and Catholic teaching on the ministry".[14] This conviction, which would have amazed older commentators (who had a special fondness for oppositions) is gradually being accepted today in ecumenical groups, and it won the support of ours. How can we fail to rejoice at this?

3. The Apostolic Succession

There has been new thinking on this criterion in recent years. What is primary in the apostolic succession is not the gesture of the laying on of hands by a bishop, but what this gesture signifies: "*a particular content* in which conformity with the apostolic tradition holds first place".[15] This judgment of Père Congar's expresses the authentic Christian tradition from *1 Clement* to Thomas Aquinas. Faith, the call of Christ, the bestowal of a charism of the Spirit for the service of the community, all these are prior conditions for the efficacy of the rite of the laying on of hands. The legalism which dominated the Western Church

[12] And so an effective sign of grace. Cf. *Institutes* IV, 19. 28: "I am not opposed to accepting it (the laying on of hands) as a sacrament." Nevertheless, Calvin did not use the word because "it is neither ordinary nor common among the faithful." He was also suspicious of it because of its implications of superstition. Cf. L. Schummer, *op. cit.*, pp. 36–96.

[13] *Sacerdoce et ministère*, ch. IV, "L'ordination au ministère".

[14] In the two books mentioned in note 1. In the second, a sequel to the first, the author is even more favourable to Calvin. He explains this as the result of "*retractationes*" on the part of the research worker, and also of "the more rapid evolution of ecumenical theology in the last few years".

[15] Y. M. J. Congar, "Apostolicité du ministère et apostolicité de doctrine, réaction protestante et tradition catholique", *Volk Gottes, Festgabe für Josef Höfer* (Freiburg, 1967), pp. 84–110.

from the time of Gregory VII produced an unfortunate reversal of poles, and the gesture of the laying on of hands remained in practice the only criterion of legitimate apostolic succession.

The reformers had a lively awareness of a vocation as coming from *above* and of the preparation of the candidate by the Spirit. Since they could no longer employ the laying on of hands by a bishop, they had to turn to a charismatic Church structure in which the whole community, through the laying on of hands by the ministers, gave itself ministers whom the Holy Spirit had prepared and marked out. In the beginning, however, they were not indifferent to the apostolic significance of the laying on of hands; since they could not receive this from the episcopal line they sought it from the presbyteral, and priests who had gone over to the Reformation made the connection. In the state of emergency which then existed, they were quite convinced that Christ, the supreme head of the Church (shaken then by such a crisis) would supply anything they might lack. When Vatican II today recognizes a certain ecclesial character in the Protestant communities, this in itself is evidence of a certain apostolic character in their ministry. This apostolic character, finally, is being renewed.

In extreme cases, of course, Calvin admitted the validity of a purely charismatic ministry (without the laying on of hands). But in extreme cases (such as a state of extreme emergency) our own post-conciliar theology can make no firm rule. Having been forced to broaden its teaching on the sacraments, it would no longer dare to set legal limits to the action of the Spirit and his mysterious ways of supplying for deficiencies. Serious theologians in our group are quite prepared to admit such a possibility.

This summary account is based, on the Catholic side, on the possibilities opened up by Vatican II and, on the Protestant side, on a reconsideration of Calvin's positions interpreted with a view to possible reconciliation between the churches. On both sides, the "other side" has been given the most generous possible interpretation, as is only fitting; while we remain completely faithful to the norms of our churches, we have a sense of meeting at a deeper level.

*   *   *

From the "practical" point of view, I feel that the difficulties would be covered by a liturgy of reconciliation made up as follows:[16]

1. *A double ecclesial "metanoia".* Our Western Church has been injured as the result of the actions of both sides, those who remained and those who were forced to leave. The first act of reconciliation would therefore be a bilateral confession which would wipe out, at the foot of the cross, a past which is so painful. These two examinations of conscience have never so far been worked out in detail, nor, *a fortiori*, have they been followed by the double confession. This first act is indispensable.

2. *A common epiclesis,* humble and fervent, begging the Holy Spirit to make up our deficiencies (the principle of compensation and "economy"), to unite and mutually enrich our complementarities and make us ready for a common celebration.

3. *A reciprocal laying on of hands* as a (traditional) sign of forgiveness and mission. It would be necessary for the priests to include the bishop of the local church, since it is his function to take responsibility for such an action. Our brother ministers would have to decide how their synod would be represented.

4. There could then be a *celebration of the Eucharist,* according to one of the forms of the new liturgy—which is not "Protestant", as its opponents say, but completely satisfies the demands of ecumenism.

It goes without saying that the proposed solution would only be put into operation with the agreement of our respective authorities, as an experiment and an *example* to which further discussion could refer.

Translated by Francis McDonagh

---

[16] This schema, given here in summary form, was presented for the first time to the Les Dombes group by Père Sesboüé, S.J. in 1968.

Walter Kasper

Convergence and Divergence in the Question of Office

I. The New Situation

DESPITE the many painful divergences that still remain, what emerges most strikingly from the contributions to this theme is that there is a great measure of convergence. The attitude of the churches, even towards the difficult question of office, has clearly undergone a heartening change. The experience of the active presence of the Holy Spirit in all the churches and of their mutual solidarity in the one Spirit, officially confirmed by the Second Vatican Council, was bound to lead eventually to the question of office. Since the service of the Word and Sacrament is carried out in a special way in and through the offices of the different churches, is the Holy Spirit not active, Christians have inevitably been asking, in these offices? If we take the experience of the churches at all seriously, we can no longer repeat the old, confessional arguments. We are bound to take as our point of departure the presence of office as a spiritual and concrete reality in the other churches, although each has, of course, to be defined theologically.

This understanding of office is based on experience and at once precludes two possible solutions to the problem. On the one hand, we can no longer require other Christians to renounce their erroneous ideas and accept re-ordination. On the other hand, we cannot just leap over the hurdles that still stand in our way and pretend that the problem no longer exists. It is not enough simply to point to a possible and, as everyone now recognizes, necessary plurality of structures in office. Pluralism is meaningful and not just a euphemism for chaos and contradiction only when it relates to a common denominator. There is therefore only one course of action open to us. We must take this new experience very seriously, reconsider the conflicting traditions concerning office in the different churches in this light and look carefully for new ways ahead.

If this is the right course to follow, we can no longer accept the criteria of validity which were applied in the past to Catholic, Orthodox and Anglican orders as the only ones. These can only serve now as signs to help us to recognize where and in what way the Spirit is active in the different churches. They are signs of life, not life itself. We have also to take other signs into account and treat them as equally important. Ultimately, what we have to do is to use spiritual judgment and to differentiate between spirits. The new situation requires us to study the whole question of office in the churches in the wider theological context of Christ, the Spirit and the Church.

II. New Points of View

If this is done, a whole new range of points of view is revealed. Some of these have been discussed in the preceding articles on this theme. I should like to deal very briefly here with three of the most important of them.

(a) The point of view of the local church and collegiality. The Church is made present not only as the universal Church, but also as the local eucharistic community of believers, which is not simply a branch or "urban" or "rural" district of the Church as a whole. This means that the question of the recognition of office should be explored at the level of the local churches, in which there may be completely different structures of office. The unity of the universal Church is to be found in the community of the local churches and in mutual recognition of their offices. Without these, the local church is in danger of becoming a sect. This approach to the problem of office from the level of the local churches should be a very fruitful one.

(b) Baptism, the Eucharist and office in the Church. Mutual recognition of baptism is one of the most important elements in the ecumenical movement. Baptism is not an isolated event. The baptized person is incorporated into the *one* Church and his baptism points to the Eucharist as the highest activity of the Church. The mutual recognition of the baptism and the ecclesial character of other churches therefore inevitably tends towards a mutual recognition and an eventual sharing of the Eucharist. But a prior condition for the carrying out of baptism and the Eucharist is office. This means that mutual recognition of the ecclesial character of other churches would be inconsistent if the offices of those churches were not at the same time recognized, although each of them has, of course, to be subjected to a detailed theological interpretation. It is, however, simply not possible to give with one hand what one takes away with the other.

(c) The historical character of the Church. The Church is on the way between Easter and the *parousia*, and none of the existing churches can identify itself with the perfect Church. Since the Church has to accomplish its mission in history, then, and since it has to confess its own sinfulness and rely constantly on God's mercy, it can never apply its canon law in all its severity, but only a law of grace. This point of view is represented in the Eastern Church by the principle of *oikonomia* and in the West by the principle of *supplet ecclesia* and the practice of dispensation. As far as the question of the recognition of office in other churches is concerned, we may conclude that God's work can often be carried out in spite of defective structures, that it can adapt itself to changing historical circumstances, and that portentous historical events are all subject to God's grace and forgiveness. This is why an individual ordination cannot be regarded as an isolated event. It has rather to be understood within the total framework of history and of the faith of the Church.

III. NEW QUESTIONS

The earlier differences have not simply been done away with in the light of these new points of view. They can, on the contrary, be seen in a new light, and this in itself reveals new questions to which no final answers can as yet be given. The main difference that still remains is that between those churches which insist on the apostolic succession of office in the sense of an uninterrupted chain of imposition of hands, and those which regard this sign as possibly valuable under certain circumstances, but as basically dispensable.

The most urgent of the questions which Protestant Christians will ask is whether this apostolic succession is not as important a sign today as it was in the past. The opinion is gaining ground among theologians generally that man's freedom and his adhesion to legal forms do not necessarily have to be diametrically opposed to each other. Legal forms can, on the contrary, help to act as a brake on an exuberance of spirit and the possible consequence of this, which is not a sign of the Spirit, but a sign of confusion. The fundamental question, then, is: What value is placed on this sign?

The theological value that is placed on this sign is also a fundamental question for Christians of the Catholic tradition nowadays. Yves Congar especially has shown that the idea of apostolic succession was originally and even until the high Middle Ages primarily a succession in apostolic faith and love, succession in the sense of uninterrupted imposition of hands being no more than a sign which lost its power as soon as the one holding office lost the apostolic faith by heresy. Apostolic succession in the narrower sense cannot therefore be regarded as a guarantee. The bishop's imposition of hands is therefore only a sign that the office-bearer is in communion with the apostolic Church.

The change from this notion of apostolic succession to that based on rather formal criteria of validity came about as a result of the change of attitude which the Church underwent between the first and second millennia. After the first thousand years or so of the Church's history, interest was no longer centred upon the activity of God made present in the office of the Church. The analytically-minded theologians of the scholastic period were more interested in the inner structure of the sacramental signs, their efficacy and validity. They thus gave more prominence to the task of establishing criteria of validity which could be applied to the Church's office. The result was a new and epoch-making form, not only of the Church itself, but of its theology and office. We cannot reverse this situation today, but we can ask ourselves whether, as we move from the second into the third millennium, the Church will perhaps not adopt another new and epoch-making form. Will this new form perhaps be closer to its origins and more open to charismatic aspects of Christian life?

No definitive answer has been given to these questions in the various articles on this theme. What the authors have shown, however, is that the question of office, which so many Christians believe to be the one unsolved problem of ecumenical dialogue, is being approached from all sides with great vigour, and that various new solutions are being suggested. Certainly the disagreement which, it is often claimed, exists with regard to the question of office can no longer be used to conceal a reluctance to move forward in ecumenical discussion.

What is of decisive importance in the mutual recognition of different offices is not primarily the question of criteria of validity, but that of a basic consensus of theological understanding. Each church has, of course, to confer office in its own way, but history shows us how subject to change this form can be. Priests have been ordained by priests, and the imposition of hands was not made the constitutive form of conferring a valid office until quite recently, by Pius XII. It cannot therefore be applied in every case as the sole criterion for all churches at all times.

I believe that the only indispensable criteria for the recognition of other offices are those which apply to the "differentiation of spirits"—the confession of true faith and proven value in service for the community. Provided both of these are present, the question of office need no longer be an obstacle to ecumenical dialogue, but can be set free from the theological isolation that has for so long surrounded it. If office in the Church is a true expression of the Gospel in and for the community and if it serves to build up the Church, there can be no theological objection to a mutual recognition of offices.

Translated by David Smith

PART II
DOCUMENTATION

Inter-Church Dialogue about Office

1. *Catholics and Lutherans*

Harding Meyer

ALMOST simultaneously two groups of Catholics and Lutherans recently held talks on the subject of "Office and the Recognition of Office". One group consisted of the United States National Committee of the World Association of Lutherans and the American Bishops' Commission for Ecumenical and Inter-denominational Affairs. I have called this group the "USA Dialogue".[1] The other was the group which the World Association of Lutherans and the Roman Catholic Church call the *International Study Commission on the Gospel and the Church*. I have referred to this group as the "Study Commission".[2]

Although there was cross-representation in both talks, and mutual information was provided, the two groups worked in the main independently of each other and came to their own separate conclusions.

The USA Dialogue (dating from 1965) had, at its third and fourth session, considered questions relating to the Last Supper and its meaning. This group had reached a quite considerable consensus about the real presence of Christ and the sacrificial character of the Eucharist. But the now pressing question of intercommunion was abandoned after a first session on the subject: it was realized that this question could not be resolved

---

[1] Events, votes and report on the talks in: *Lutherans and Catholics in Dialogue IV: Eucharist and Ministry* (1970).
[2] The final Report of the Study Commission has not so far (October 1971) been publicly released. But the main results of the discussion on office are given in the final Report on the third session of the Study Commission, published, with a detailed commentary, in *Lutherische Rundschau/Lutheran World* (1971/2).

without first considering that of office. In the USA Dialogue discussions on office came to concentrate from the beginning more particularly on the *eucharistic office*.

The Study Commission, on the other hand, dealt more extensively with the question of the Gospel and its handing down. Already at the first session in 1967, all the participants had agreed on a joint statement which they regarded as basic: that the authority of the Church can only be service of the word which, as the word of the Lord, remains inviolable. This statement, which uses the concept "word" in the sense of "Gospel", became the recurrent theme in the discussions on office. And office was taken to mean "service to the Gospel".

The distinction arising out of these differences in perspective in the treatment of the idea of office are quite obvious, but they canot be described in detail here.

If we take a look at the results of the talks, we must differentiate between statements of "consensus" in which people really spoke in unison, and statements of "convergence" in which they spoke with different voices but with a common intention and with movement towards each other. Here it is important to note that, making all due allowances for the convictions of the participants, "converging" statements should in their own way be able to remove contradictions, and to make fellowship possible.

Consensus was arrived at in the two talks on the following points:

The "office" or "ministry of reconciliation" (2 Cor. 5. 18) is a constituent part of God's work of reconciliation in Christ. This service is the work of the whole Church.

At the same time there has existed from the Church's beginnings a special office that is part of the community and stands together with the community under Christ, and yet at the same time is in Christ's place and stands vis-à-vis the community.

This office dates back to the Church's apostolic origin and it is there that it finds its norm.

But reference back to the Church's origin can also be found in various official structures. We must differentiate between permanent basic structures or fundamental truth, and the structural variations of office. This opens up the possibility of finding responsible new forms for outmoded official structures.

The participants did not of course attempt to defuse the really controversial questions by forming them into consensus rather than convergence statements.

1. Apostolic Succession

The teaching of the Church's descent from the apostles was uniformly affirmed in its basic intention. This apostolic origin of the Church was primarily seen as the continuity of the apostolic Gospel, so that it was true in the most real and most important sense that the whole Church stood in the apostolic succession. Apostolic succession in the narrower sense—as the unbroken succession of bishops—was seen as sign and aspect, but not as a *sine qua non* or guarantee of the apostolicity of the Church and its office. There were, of course, many differences in the importance and value given to this sign.

2. Ordination as Sacrament

Both reports agree on a positive convergence, in so far as the decisive question whether ordination confers a grace of office and the Holy Spirit is invoked, was answered in the affirmative by the Lutherans. But we must not overlook the fact that there was disagreement among the Lutherans of the Study Commission on this question, so that the Report, while referring to the practice of ordination in the Lutheran Church (the laying on of hands and invoking of the Holy Spirit), says very little on how this practice is to be understood.

3. Indelible Character

Faced by a one-sided ontological or metaphysical understanding of "character", the Catholic participants were strictly functional in their explanation: It was a matter of the office vis-à-vis the community, and at the same time of the absolute character of ordination—the fact that it cannot be repeated. This explanation accords with the Lutheran concept of office and practice, although the unrepeatability of ordination was not as positively affirmed by the Lutherans of the Study Commission as it seems to have been by those in the USA Dialogue. The Report of the Study Commission confines itself as before to pointing out that re-ordination forms no part of the existing Lutheran practice of ordination.

4. *Recognition of Office*

Both groups made it clear that this question has a different meaning for Lutherans and for Catholics. For this reason Catholics and Lutherans produced separate arguments and recommendations in their two reports.

Even if one cannot go so far as to say that the question of validity, legitimacy and recognition of office was totally unknown to Lutherans, it remains true that for them this question is ultimately contained in the question of the correct preaching of the Gospel. The decisive reason for the Lutheran recommendation to their churches that they recognize the office of the Catholic Church (USA Dialogue) or seriously consider the question of recognition (Study Commission) is shown to be the agreement already arrived at on the understanding of the Gospel and the administration of sacraments. The Lutherans of the Study Commission went further than those of the USA Dialogue. The former saw in the already expressed agreement on gospel understanding the possibility of (at least "occasional") joint appearances in the pulpit and on the altar. In the USA Dialogue, this question is still explicitly avoided by Lutherans and Catholics alike.

The position taken up by the Catholic participants was clearly different—from the point of view of the discussion and the line taken in the discussion. They used stronger arguments whose chief aim was to weaken the traditional Catholic criticism of deficiency in the Lutheran office as such. The individual arguments can only be listed here:

Insights derived from biblical exegesis and historical studies as to the "openness" of the New Testament and early patristic witness in regard to the ordering of churches and the structure of ministries—the possibility of presbyter ordination and succession—the necessity of a more extensive and deeper understanding of apostolic succession.

Recognition of the ecclesial character of other churches (Vatican II) as the theological foundation for a recognition of offices.

Agreements and convergences in understanding on the subject of ecclesiastical office.

The possibility of establishing valid office through charismatic commission and pneumatic development in a situation of need (only in the Study Commission).

The presence of the correct intention at the Lutheran celebration of the eucharistic meal (only in the USA Dialogue).

A new interpretation of the teachings of Trent on office and ordination, particularly canon 7 and canon 10 of the seventh and twenty-third sessions respectively (only in the USA Dialogue).

The Catholc participants in both talks did not go so far as to recommend to the authorities of their own Church a formal recognition of the Lutheran office. Instead they energetically pressed the question whether, in the light of the given arguments, and in view of ecumenical endeavours at the present moment, a recognition of the Lutheran office was not to be recommended (USA Dialogue) or seriously considered (Study Commission).

Translated by Erika Young

2. *Ministry and its Recognition in Anglican-Roman Catholic Dialogue*

Herbert Ryan

THE question of ministry and its recognition has been treated by the Joint Commission on Anglican-Roman Catholic Relations in the United States (ARC), the Anglican-Roman Catholic Preparatory Commission and its successor the Anglican-Roman Catholic International Commission (ARCIC). From the experience of six years of dialogue this problem is seen to involve the task of discovering whether a real oneness in faith exists at present between the Anglican Communion and the Roman Catholic

Church on three points: the nature of the Church, the meaning of ministry and the understanding of Eucharist. Agreement in the faith on these issues is the fundamental prerequisite to the mutual recognition of ministry. If Roman Catholics and Anglicans can mutually agree on what they believe themselves to be as Church and what actually they possess in the ministry, then the theological foundation for the mutual recognition of ministry has been laid. The canonical or liturgical expression of this discovery of oneness in the faith should be consonant with the new and mutually shared theological conviction that both the Roman Catholic Church and the churches of the Anglican Communion share fully in the reality of the one Church.

I. Old Problems—New Questions

Not surprisingly the major difficulties experienced in Anglican-Roman Catholic dialogue about ministry focus on the adverse judgment concerning the validity of Anglican orders passed by Leo XIII in *Apostolicae Curae* and the relationship between the Petrine office and the papal ministry. Though neither of these problems has been solved by the dialogue, new ways of approaching them have been suggested. These new approaches spring from the experience of the dialogue itself and are contained in the working paper "The Church and Ministry" composed at the second meeting of ARCIC at Venice in September 1970. To deal with the problems raised by the bull *Apostolicae Curae* the working paper does not envision a full-scale historical study which would review from the time of the sixteenth century the question of the validity of Anglican orders. Rather it asks for a thorough theological examination of the presuppositions which were operative in the document and for a judgment upon them in the light of the development of Roman Catholic doctrine on the Church and ministry from 1896 to the present. What is called for is an exercise in theological understanding to see what perennial value *Apostolicae Curae* may possess. In treating of the problem of the relationship of the Petrine office and the papal ministry the working paper raises the question of whether or not in the light of modern exegesis there is not a basis in the New Testament itself for speaking of a Petrine office, peculiar to Peter himself, within the apostolic college and community. In relating the Petrine office to the papal ministry the working paper suggests that the Roman primacy may reflect the model of the original Petrine office by imitation if not by direct succession.

Though *Apostolicae Curae* and papal ministry constitute major difficulties between the Roman Catholic Church and the Anglican Communion, there is truly a profound and extensive common understanding among Roman and Anglican theologians on the nature of ministry. The ARCIC working paper is ample evidence of this. Yet the difficulties are real and wishing them to go away will not make them vanish. The ARCIC working paper poignantly describes the situation. "It is sad that Anglicans and Roman Catholics, while sharing deep understanding of the *nature* of ministry, differ on the question of where full and true ministry may be found."

II. The Dialogue since 1965

Hopefully the new approaches to the old problems of *Apostolicae Curae* and papal ministry may contribute to solving the question of where full and true ministry may be found. How did these new approaches arise? This brief article will sketch the history of how during the course of six years of dialogue between the Roman Catholic Church and the Anglican Communion the new approaches slowly emerged.

The first meeting of ARC in June 1965 discussed the theology of the sacraments of Baptism and Confirmation. No theological difference between a Roman Catholic and Anglican understanding of these sacraments was uncovered. A firm foundation appeared for the mutual recognition of the baptismal ministry of members of the Roman Catholic Church and the Episcopal Church. In February 1966, the second meeting of ARC uncovered considerable agreement on the theology of the Eucharist. So much agreement on the Eucharist has been reached that the question was raised why the Roman and Episcopalian members of ARC could not share the Eucharist together. Both parties were in accord that it was the present division between the Roman Catholic Church and the Anglican Communion in carrying out the Church's mission to the world that constituted the fundamental barrier to sharing the Eucharist together. The reasons for this division were fundamentally the lack of "collegiality" between the Anglican and Roman bishops and the adverse judgment of *Apostolicae Curae* concerning the validity of Anglican orders. It was suggested despite this official adverse judgment one could not deny the reality and fruitfulness of Anglican ministry. Thus for the first time in ARC the problem of the mutual recognition of the ordained ministry appeared. The problem had a context much wider than that of the theology which underlay *Apostolicae Curae*. ARC was asking a new question: How can one understand theologically the reality of Anglican ministry today?

In October 1966 the third meeting of ARC discussed the function of the minister in the eucharistic celebration. The dialogue showed that both the Episcopal Church and the Roman Catholic Church hold firmly for the necessity of an ordained ministry in which the three orders of bishops, priests (presbyters) and deacons are included. During this meeting a method was proposed to explore together the theology of the ordained ministry. Rather than engage in historical studies of the Reformation period to see if the adverse judgment of *Apostolicae Curae* on the existence of the sacrament of Orders in the Anglican Communion was justified, it was agreed to see if the two churches shared the same theological understanding of the ordained ministry in its relation to the Church as a eucharistic community. The subsequent meetings of ARC investigated the nature of eucharistic sacrifice and concentrated on the study of the functions of the ordained ministry, especially the bishop, in the hope of showing that an agreement in faith on these points does actually exist between the Episcopal Church and the Roman Catholic Church.

The experience of the ARC dialogue seems to have influenced the discussion of ministry during the meetings of the Anglican-Roman Catholic Joint Preparatory Commission. The report which this Commission composed at its final meeting in Malta in January 1968 echoes the thinking of the third ARC meeting:

We are agreed that among the conditions required for intercommunion are both a true sharing in faith and the mutual recognition of ministry. The latter presents a particular difficulty in regard to Anglican Orders according to the traditional judgment of the Roman Church. We believe that the present growing together of our two Communions and the needs of the future require of us a very serious consideration of this question in the light of modern theology. The theology of the ministry forms part of the theology of the Church and must be considered as such. It is only when sufficient agreement has been reached as to the nature of the priesthood and the meaning to be attached in this context to the word "validity" that we could proceed, working always jointly, to the application of this doctrine to the Anglican ministry of today. We would wish to re-examine historical events and past documents only to the extent that they can throw light upon the facts of the present situation.[1]

When ARCIC, which succeeded the Anglican-Roman Catholic Preparatory Commission, met at Windsor in January 1970, one set of papers prepared before the meeting explored the topic of Eucharist and Ministry. After a general discussion of all the preparatory papers the members of ARCIC divided themselves into three drafting groups and produced schemata for further work on three related topics: The Church and Authority, The Church and Eucharist and The Church and Ministry. The set of preparatory papers had dealt primarily with Ministry in relation to the Eucharist, but the schemata produced at Windsor for further work by ARCIC corresponded more closely to the programme outlined in the Malta report.

The second section of the schema on the Church and Ministry was entitled "Ministry in a Divided Church". It dealt with the problem of the validity of Anglican orders and concluded with two paragraphs on the renewal of Anglican and Roman Catholic ministry. The schema repudiated an historical investigation of the problem of Anglican orders and asserted that such an investigation inevitably leads to an impasse. Further work on

---

[1] Report of the Anglican-Roman Catholic Joint Preparatory Commission, *Lambeth Conference 1968 Documents on Anglican-Roman Catholic Relations* (Saffron Walden, Essex, 1968),, p. 19.

the second section of this schema was assigned to a subcommittee of the ARCIC members from the United States.

Among other topics the eighth meeting of ARC in June 1970 discussed ministry in a divided church. ARC reiterated its belief that the mutual recognition of ministry depended on a prior shared theological understanding of the ordained ministry in the Anglican Communion and the papal ministry. Collaborative theological work should be done in order to see how Anglicans could commend their ordained ministry to the Roman Catholic Church and how Romans could offer the papal ministry to the Anglican Communion.

III. Theological Consequences in a New Pastoral Situation

The ARCIC working paper on The Church and Ministry owes much to the subcommittee report originating in the eighth ARC meeting. The subcommittee report submitted to the Venice meeting of ARCIC in September 1970 stressed the fact that a new pastoral situation existed in which Anglicans and Romans were aware of their sharing the baptismal ministry, were actively engaged together in works of spiritual ecumenism and desired a closer union in order to fulfil together the Church's mission of service to the world. Could one see the theological significance of this new pastoral situation as an urging by the Holy Spirit to seek for new solutions to the old problems of Anglican orders and papal ministry? By fostering even closer cooperation between Romans and Anglicans in carrying out the Church's programme of service to the world the lingering atmosphere of old hurt and past polemics could be still further cleared. If this were done, what principles could be mutually agreed on to aid Romans and Anglicans in their theological self-understanding of the ordained ministry, the commendation of Anglican ministry to the Roman Catholic Church and its acceptance by the Roman Catholic Church? To find these principles one would have to examine the theological presuppositions operative in *Apostolicae Curae* in the light of contemporary Roman Catholic doctrine, to indicate the development of Roman Catholic doctrine on the ordained ministry since 1896 and to see if this doctrine is acceptable to Anglicans.

The ARCIC working paper puts the matter succinctly.

The *nature of the study* we would recommend here would be circumscribed historically and theologically: *historically* it would involve tracing which of the arguments from the Roman Commission of 1896 found their way into the bull *Apostolicae Curae*; *theologically* it would involve (a) analysing the arguments to see what the theological assumptions behind them were, (b) examining whether Roman Catholic theology can show a genuine and consistent development of doctrine with regard to those assumptions from 1896 to the present.

This study would be a contribution to that wider judgment which we hope will eventually be made—whether there is sufficient doctrinal convergence between the Roman Catholic Church and the Anglican Communion to permit them to see one another as sharing fully in the reality of the one Church.[2]

[2] Anglican-Roman Catholic Working Papers, *Catholic Mind*, Vol. 69, No. 1252 (April 1971), p. 45.

3. *Interdenominational Dialogue in France (Les Dombes)*

Hébert Roux

I. History and Character of the Dialogue

THE "Les Dombes" interdenominational discussion group can already draw on a considerable experience. Founded in 1937 on the initiative of the Abbé Paul Couturier, it has tried to remain faithful to the basic inspiration of that promoter of spiritual ecumenism while making use of the gradual broadening and deepening of theological dialogue in the years before and after the Council.

The group has certain characteristic features which help to situate it in relation to others and to explain its concern with the conditions for a full restoration of ecclesial communion on the level of the ministry and the sacraments.

1. *The group is the result of a private initiative*, and has no official "mandate". It is made up of equal numbers of Catholics and Protestants from France and Switzerland who meet each year in response to a personal invitation issued by a standing committee. This has enabled it to preserve a relative homogeneity favourable to the development of mutual acquaintance and understanding, and to establish a certain continuity in the development of its work while retaining complete freedom in the choice of subjects for study and in methodology. During each meeting "common theses" are drawn up on the basis of papers from each side which have been discussed by the group. These theses note the points of agreement or disagreement and outline the course of subsequent research. They are binding only on participants, and are in principle solely for internal use, though they have received some attention from outside, from the French ecclesiastical authorities, and from other research groups.

2. "Because we are making a common effort to work fruitfully in the field of theology, at the risk of betraying our mission we cannot approach dogmatic mysteries without also praying together. God will only enlighten our work in common if we ask him to, in common. We have experimental evidence of this." Those were the words of the Abbé Couturier when he summed up the results of the first ten years of the group's life in 1948. The evidence has been strengthened since then, as a testimony to the inseparability of prayer and theology as two complementary aspects of the same approach of *fidens quaerens intellectum*.

3. *Close co-operation has been established in our work between the ministry of doctors and that of pastors.* The papers are usually presented by theologians, but priests and ministers with direct responsibilities in the ecumenical pastoral work of our churches take an active part in the discussion and the drawing up of the theses.[1] The particular situation of theology in France gives it "a character which is more pastoral than theor-

---

[1] The theses for the years 1956 to 1964 were published with a commentary in *Verbum Caro* 70, and those for 1965–1970 in the "Pages Documentaires" of *Unité Chrétienne* 23 (Lyons, July 1971).

etical", makes it work "more closely with the grass roots" and anxious to be "of direct use to the Christian people".[2] We take it for granted that doctrinal study of the conditions necessary for full ecclesial communion—study concentrating on the eucharistic mystery and the recognition of ministries—cannot be unrelated either to the facts which characterize the faith and the sacramental and ministerial life of the local churches or to the duty to inform and enlighten the competent episcopal and synodal authorities.[3]

4. Let us finally emphasize the multi-disciplinary character of our work. For each subject chosen we call on specialists in exegesis, history, patrology and dogmatic theology from various Catholic and Protestant faculties and institutes. Such a confrontation brings out different aspects of the subjects, gives a better appreciation of the historical context of traditional doctrinal formulations, and, finally, by renewing the dynamism of faith, contributes in many cases to a rediscovery or a deeper awareness of important "points of agreement on essentials".

II. The Content of the Dialogue

There is no room here to give a full account of the ground we have covered or a complete list of the points of agreement established. We will simply note some of the more important stages, beginning with a series of studies on "The Church and the Holy Spirit" (1965–66), which have brought us to the current problems of "intercommunion" and in particular to the problem of the recognition of ministries.

"The mystery of the Trinity is revealed in the economy and is inseparable from it; any understanding of it which wants to remain an understanding in faith must remain constantly rooted in the economy. Speculation on the Trinity in itself...involves faith in serious spiritual dangers." It is the economy taken in its totality, according to Scripture, which reveals to us the person

[2] See Y. Congar, "Situation présente de la théologie en France", in *La Croix*, 31 March 1971 and 3 April 1971.
[3] A note attached to the 1967 theses makes this point: "The only aim of our work is to serve our churches and to put forward elements for a solution to the responsible authorities in our communities."

of the Holy Spirit in his relations with the Father and the Son, by making us aware of his essential role in our participation in the mystery. In particular, it is essential to develop pneumatology in close connection with all aspects of Christology (1965).

"A critical examination of Western theologies (Catholic and Protestant) shows that this norm of the economy has not always been respected. Among the signs of this are the understanding of sanctification in a too individualistic sense, the neglect of the role of the Holy Spirit in creation and eschatology and of his mission in relation to the resurrection and pentecost, and an over-emphasis on Christ's priestly office to the detriment of his royal and prophetic offices, etc.

"The attitude which automatically submits all the data of faith to an examination of the substance of the Gospel in a living relation to the person of Christ through the action of the Holy Spirit throws a new light on our respective positions. . . . It gives an axis and a dynamism to the search for unity and directs us towards intercommunion in the truth" (1967).

From this viewpoint it becomes possible to clarify the area of agreement and reduce the area of disagreement between our churches, as regards both the content of eucharistic doctrine itself and the understanding of the eucharistic mystery as the sacrament of ecclesial unity in relation to the doctrine of ministries and apostolic succession.

III. MINISTRIES AND THE APOSTOLIC SUCCESSION

On this last point I give below the essence of the 1968 theses:

"1. This succession must be understood in the context of the permanence of the Church as a whole, founded on the apostles, the witnesses and stewards of the redemptive work of Christ, which bears, in the continuity of history, the responsibility for proclaiming the Gospel to the world. This succession is attested and symbolized by the continuity of the elements of the apostolic charge which can be handed on . . . entrusted to ministers instituted by the Lord, called by his Spirit and received and ordained in the Church.

"2. The fullness of the apostolic succession implies a continuity in the transmission of the ministerial charge, faithfulness to the preaching and teaching of the apostles, a life in conformity with the Gospel and the demands of the mission. In other words, the succession, as a visible sign, bears witness to the apostolic character of the Church. . . .

"3. The Lord appoints men to the ministry which he instituted himself and gives them to his Church, which is called to recognize them in the Spirit and to do its part by ordaining them. If this discernment is performed by the whole community the ordination itself, the sacramental character of which none of us disputes, is the fact of the pastoral college.

"4. By means of this ordination men are appointed to be, in the name of Christ and through the life-giving action of the Holy Spirit, in the continuity of the universal Church, ministers of the word and sacraments, shepherds of the flock and guardians of its unity for the sake of its mission in the world.

"5. . . . The apostolic succession may be obscured in one or other of its elements without this being a reason for us to doubt Christ's faithfulness to his Church. We believe that this faithfulness can, through the Spirit, raise up extraordinary forms of ministry which act as a prophetic summons to the regeneration of the Church. . . ."

We felt that these theses constituted a step towards a mutual recognition of ministries in spite of remaining difficulties, and open the way, in conditions to be worked out on the basis of a sufficient eucharistic faith, for really meaningful common celebrations, bearing in mind "the urgent missionary needs of our time". The 1969 and 1970 theses mark a deepening of the doctrine of ministries in a more sharply pneumatological perspective. "The exercise of any ministry (institutional or charismatic) must always be animated by the same Spirit, in the service of the *koinōnia*. . . We cannot reach unity through theological agreement alone. An *ecclesial* conversion (*metanoia*) is needed. One stage in this conversion must be the reconciliation of ministries. . . . This reconciliation must be given sacramental expression . . . for example, a mutual laying on of hands performed as a gesture of reconciliation and epiclesis."

Finally, at the same time, in "requests" addressed to the Churches, in 1969 the Les Dombes group emphasized the urgent need to study possible approaches towards a common Eucharist.

By persisting in dilatory attitudes, it argued, the churches were in practice disparaging the action of the Spirit in the (sometimes mixed) aspirations of many of the faithful. In 1970, in a study of the Church as "the communion of saints" and of the relation between the universal Church and the local church, the group made specific suggestions of points connected with the exercise of the ministry and church structures at which ecclesial *metanoia* could operate as a matter of priority, on both the Catholic and the Protestant sides.[4] It is certain that work in this direction has hardly begun; if it is to go further there must be a new awareness in the communities of the Spirit's appeal to the churches for repentance.[5]

Translated by Francis McDonagh

[4] Cf. B. Sesboüé, "Situation de l'oecuménisme", in *Croire aujourd'hui* (January 1971).
[5] The purpose of the 1971 Les Dombes meeting is to work out an agreed doctrinal and pastoral text on the Eucharist.

4. *Anglican-Methodist Dialogue on the Unification of Ministries*

John Macquarrie

I. Two Different Types of Ministry

THE implications of the Anglican-Methodist dialogue on ministry in England have significance far beyond that country, for the problem of ministry in this case is one that will have to be faced in many other situations. It is the problem of bringing together a Catholic-type ministry on the one side with a Protestant-type ministry on the other. The Anglican ministry has preserved the classic threefold ordering of bishops, priests and deacons, and it stands not only in the succession of apostolic truth but in that visible, personal, historical succession which it traces back through its bishops to St Augustine, founder of the see of Canterbury, and through him to the earliest ministry of the Church. The Methodist ministry, on the other hand, originated in the late eighteenth century, and while it claims to be an effective ministry of Christ, it makes no claim to stand in that historic succession or to exhibit that classic form which are to be seen in Anglicanism.

Anglicans do not deny the reality and effectiveness of the Methodist ministry, and they recognize that the fact that this ministry has developed outside of the mainstream of English Christianity is, in some degree at least, due to the intransigency and inflexibility of Anglicans in the past. They do not deny either that the Methodist ministry has continued to witness to apostolic truth, and that it has a genuine participation in the ministry and priesthood of Christ. But before this ministry can be fully recognized by Anglicans, it must be fully and visibly integrated into that classical form of ministry and in that historical personal succession which constitutes an essential element in Catholic ecclesiology. To be sure, there are many views held among Anglicans, and some of the more evangelical and liberal Anglicans would say that episcopacy is not essential, even though they value it highly. But in the Anglican-Methodist conversations, it has been acknowledged that liberty of interpretation concerning the nature of episcopacy "is only possible within the strictest invariability of episcopal ordination. For, while it is possible to hold a 'low' view of episcopacy within a strict invariability of practice, it becomes impossible to hold a 'high' view when this invariability is broken." In fact, very many Anglicans (and this is certainly in accordance with the weight of Anglican teaching) will not receive Holy Communion except from ministers episcopally ordained.

II. A New Ordinal

The actual plan worked out for the unification of Anglican and Methodist ministries has two major parts, one looking to the future, the other to the existing ministries.

For the future, a new ordinal has been devised which would

be used in both churches.[1] On a date to be specified, three Methodist bishops would be consecrated, and from then on, ordinations in both churches would be according to the new forms and would be mutually recognized. For my own part, I must say that the new ordinal, with forms for the ordination of bishops, priests and deacons, appears to be (with some minor exceptions) a most excellent document, theologically sound and practically workable. I would like to see it receiving attention far beyond the shores of England.[2]

There would be no problem about the future, once Methodist bishops had been consecrated and the new ordinal were in operation. But what about the existing ministries? Many ministers now serving will still be serving in thirty years time.

The unfortunate experiences of the Church of South India have made it clear that it is not sufficient simply to throw existing ministries together without some definite visible act of unification and reconciliation. If this does not happen, the result is, to put it crudely, the co-existence of first- and second-class ministries. The former are recognized everywhere, the latter are not. This leads also to strains within the new united denomination, and the Methodists have been rightly concerned that their ministry should not become divided into the new breed of the episcopally ordained and the old breed of the non-episcopally ordained.

III. The Problem of Reconciliation

To deal with this situation, there has been devised a Service of Reconciliation. In the course of this service, it is proposed that Anglican bishops will lay hands on Methodist ministers, and that, conversely, representatives of the Methodist ministry will lay hands on their Anglican colleagues. This act will symbolize the sharing of the gifts of ministry presently given to the two churches, so that all will be equally priests in the Church of God.

[1] I have discussed this more fully in my article "The Ministry and the Proposed New Anglican-Methodist Ordinal", in *The Anglican*, vol. 25, no. 4, reprinted in *Worship*, vol. 45, no. 6.

[2] The text of the proposed ordinal is published by S.P.C.K. (London, 1968).

It seems to me that this is infinitely preferable to the South India type of scheme. Apart from the invidious distinctions to which the South India scheme inevitably gave rise, it suffered from an ecclesiological docetism. As a visible, personal, historical community, the Church needs for its unification visible, personal, historical acts. Furthermore, some definite visible act of reconciliation demands also that humility without which there can be no true reconciliation but only an outward piecing together.

It is easy enough to see the meaning of the Service of Reconciliation from the Anglican side. The real, existing ministry of the Methodist is enriched and strengthened by being integrated into the visible Catholic succession. It is not quite so easy to see what is supposed to happen when a Methodist lays hands on an Anglican—indeed, it has been suggested that it would make more sense and be more in accordance with Methodist practice if, from their side, there was simply a giving of the right hand of fellowship. This would be less confusing, but I think it is important that the Anglican should have the humility to recognize that, however it is symbolized, his own ministry can be enriched and strengthened from the Methodist side.

There has been a good deal of argument as to whether the Service of Reconciliation can be regarded as an "ordination" of the Methodist minister to the Catholic presbyterate or priesthood. It seems to me that such argument is mistaken. The Service is not an ordination, but it has some features of an ordination. If there is already (as most agree) a real effective ministry, then one should not speak of an "ordination", as this would imply the conferring of such ministry or priesthood for the first time. On the other hand, if the existing ministry is enhanced and enriched by the act, then I do not see any objection to such an expression as "supplemental ordination", if anyone wanted to use it. A committee set up to clarify some of the issues in the Anglican-Methodist scheme has recently pronounced that it is possible to regard the Service of Reconciliation as "conditional ordination". But whether many Methodists would be prepared to admit this is questionable.

At the date of writing, it seems highly improbable that the Anglican-Methodist scheme will be accepted. The main problem is the Service of Reconciliation, which is felt by many people to be too vague and capable of too many interpretations to achieve what it sets out to do. Many ministers of both churches would refuse to take part in the Service, though for different reasons. Among those willing to take part there would be so many different ways of understanding the Service that it might produce confusion rather than reconciliation. For my own part, I might be willing to close my eyes, draw a deep breath, and take the plunge, but I am very unhappy about the whole direction of the ecumenical movement. As it seems to me, most current schemes for church union are in fact ecclesiastical joinery which offend theological integrity and threaten that legitimate and hard-won pluralism which can be a richness rather than a weakness in the Christian Church. I agree with Karl Rahner that we should spend far less time in dialoguing with each other and more time studying the common problems raised for all of us by the new age. In this way, through finding common answers, we shall gradually grow closer together. But I should expect that a considerable measure of pluralism and diversity will remain, and that the kind of unity that will emerge will be on the Uniate pattern, leaving side by side different rites and even different jurisdictions, a true unity in freedom.

5. The Netherlands

Peter van Leeuwen

MUTUAL recognition of baptism was achieved in the Netherlands in 1967 and, in 1971, five churches made a joint declaration about mixed marriage. Since the end of September 1970, a dialogue about intercommunion and the mutual recognition of office has been taking place within the framework of the Dutch Council of Churches, which has been in existence since 21 June 1968. The eight churches represented are the Roman Catholic Church, the Old Catholic Church, the Dutch Reformed Church, the Calvinist-Zwinglian Reformed churches, the Evangelical Lutheran Church, the Dutch Arminian Brotherhood (Remonstrants), the Dutch Mennonite Brotherhood and the United Brethren (Moravians).

The dialogue opened with a discussion about the Eucharist and the Lord's Supper. This subject is so difficult and the views of the Christian bodies taking part are so divergent that the results have so far been meagre. The question of office in the different churches and their mutual recognition is still to be debated and no doubt very divergent views will be expressed. The extreme Protestant churches still lack confidence not only in Roman Catholicism, but in the other Reformed churches, and are not taking part in this dialogue. They form a very small minority.

I. Mutual Recognition of Office as a Consequence of Mutual Recognition of Baptism and of Open Communion

A degree of recognition of the offices of other churches is included within the present mutual recognition of baptism and the mutually accepted regulation concerning mixed marriages. This mutual recognition of baptism does not necessarily apply to individual baptisms, but to baptism administered in and by the various churches, including their official administration. The joint declaration about mixed marriages also includes a recognition of the official responsibility of the churches in preparing for and solemnizing marriages, and in joint pastoral care. We should not underestimate the ecumenical importance of this pastoral practice as a first step towards mutual recognition of office.

An important resolution, with clear consequences at the local level, was passed on 8 April 1970 by the Dutch Pastoral Council, making the following recommendation to the Roman Catholic bishops. Encouragement should be given, or at least not denied, to mutual participation in the celebration of the Eucharist and Lord's Supper of different churches, subject to certain conditions. Unity in Christ must be the basis and reason for a mixed Christian community. The office-bearers must be on all sides recognized as called by the one Lord in the one Church. Finally, there must be recognition and unanimity in faith on all sides that the same saving event, that is, the memorial of Christ's death and resurrection, is taking place.

Three things must be said in explanation. Firstly, this does not mean that every church fully recognizes the other churches as such; that is, as communities assembled round the word, the sacrament and office in the service of the world. Secondly, the experience of this rediscoverd unity can, in certain situations, play an essential part in inter-church dialogue. Thirdly, these situations refer to mixed marriages, discussion and action groups and local communities which fulfil the conditions mentioned. It should also be added that the bishops promised to consult with the other members of the Dutch Council of Churches and with the Secretariat for the Promotion of Christian Unity.

This recommendation might lead to a mutual recognition of office as such by way of a recognition of those holding office in the concrete situation of church life and the official ministry. The recommendation therefore deliberately avoids implying a general recognition of office as such in the other churches and confines itself to the question of participation in the sacramental celebrations of other churches, without speaking of full communion. In concrete situations, office in the other churches is recognized as authentic and, on this basis, Christians can participate in the life of other churches.

II. The Practical Recognition of Office by Mutual Participation in the Life of Other Churches

The Pastoral Council of the three southern provinces of the Netherlands, which has representatives from the Roman Catholic Church and from five Reformed churches, declared in November 1970 that "there is every reason for making church services as open as possible to the members of other churches who wish to participate in them". Precisely how this should be done was left to the local churches themselves.

This certainly points to a recognition of office in its concrete functions. At the same time, however, the Council expressed certain objections to the much more far-reaching recognition of the Eucharist or Lord's Supper and of office in other churches which is gaining ground in the Netherlands, and which tends towards an almost complete blurring of all distinctions between the churches. The Council insists that the separate identity of the different churches must be accepted as playing an important part in the principle of unity in pluriformity. If the tension between individual identity and unity is broken, the result may be, as history has shown, a tragic schism.

This declaration has met with agreement (concerning the "openness" to participation in the services of other churches) and with criticism (concerning the need to preserve individual distinctions). The Council replied to these reactions in May 1971. While reaffirming the principle of ecumenical openness in church services, the Council stressed that this was not the ultimate perspective in ecumenism and that it did not mean that "happy developments in local inter-church relationships, leading to a responsible search for new liturgical forms had to meet with disapproval and be checked". It is, in other words, obvious that mutual recognition of the sacrament and of office in other churches goes much further at the local level than simply participating in each other's services and tends towards a sharing of the sacrament and of office.

From what has taken place both at the Dutch Pastoral Council and at the Council representing the three southern provinces, it is in the first place clear that it is above all locally that there is mutual recognition of office in other churches. Secondly, this recognition is a practical and concrete acceptance rather than a carefully considered theological conclusion. The framework of this practical recognition is to a great extent formed by the fifteen regional and one hundred and forty-five or so local church councils. These were set up in 1965 at the close of the Second Vatican Council, have grown very rapidly since 1967 and now include both lay and office-bearing members of all the participating churches.

These new inter-church councils are, of course, very varied. Some are simply free contact groups, whereas in others there is intense and far-reaching co-operation and such a concrete mutual recognition of office and the sacraments that the frontier of participation in the services and life of other churches is quickly crossed. The discussions that take place in these councils are hardly or not at all checked by theological considerations. Many groups of a distinctively Catholic or Protestant character feel confused and even scandalized by the way in which past differences are relativized, minimized or even ignored in these inter-church councils.

As for the theology of office in the Church, a report almost entirely untheological in its approach was presented at the penultimate session of the Dutch Pastoral Council. This caused it to be severely criticized, hardly discussed at all in the Council, and not judged. All the same, this report, which was almost exclusively concerned with priestly celibacy and the role of women in the Church's ministry, influenced the debate about office in the Netherlands generally.

The report on office prepared by Dr H. Berkhof of the Dutch Reformed Church, "What is Wrong with Office in the Church?", on the other hand, is soundly based on biblical theology, but is encountering resistance in Protestant circles, especially from the more orthodox members. It does, however, reveal some promising ecumenical perspectives. Berkhof defines office in the Church, for example, as a representation of Christ and he stresses the need for openness to personal office in its supra-local and even universal form. On the other hand, he does not explicitly discuss the question of the mutual recognition of office in other churches at all.

Translated by David Smith

6. Free Ministry in the U.S.A.

Gregory Baum

A RECENT ecclesiastical development in the U.S.A. may well be symptomatic of future trends in other parts of the Catholic Church. Among the large number of priests who have resigned from the official ministry, with or without formal dispensation, there are many who continue to look upon themselves as ordained ministers, as servants in the community, as marked by a special call. Without ecclesiastical approval they continue their ministry among the Christian people.

Some of these priests have founded *The Society of Priests for a Free Ministry* (SPFM).[1] The purpose of this Society is to promote a sense of ministry among the priests who left, to give public expression to their protest against the hierarchy's indifference in regard to the social and ecclesiastical crisis in the U.S.A., to encourage experiments in alternative styles of Christian priesthood, and to carry on, if possible, a conversation with the institutional Church. The SPFM does not regard itself in any way as a sectarian movement. Its members do not deny the authority of the Catholic hierarchy nor the validity of the ordinary ministry of Catholic priests. They hold, rather, that ministry in the Church is manifold, that there should be diverse ways of exercising this priesthood, and since the present ecclesiastical government does not provide for the necessary variety, that the time has come to seek new styles of priestly life and service, without the required permission. They advocate, therefore, a free ministry.

To understand the concept of free ministry it is necessary to inquire to whom this ministry is directed. Are these priests clerics without people, invading Catholic and Protestant congregations to carve out for themselves a kingdom of their own? Are they trespassing among people well looked after by the official ministry? Or are these priests surrounded by a community in which their service is offered and received? There is, in the U.S.A., a wide and ever-growing section of the Christian community that regards itself as post-ecumenical.[2] It is made up of Christians, many of whom are Catholic, who have been involved in the reform and renewal of the churches, but whose Christian self-understanding has been so transformed that they

---

[1] For literature see *Proceedings of the First, Second and Third Annual Conventions*, available at SPFM, National Office, 4231 194th Street, Flushing, N.Y. 11358. Also see Eugene Bianchi, "The Free Ministry", *Commonweal*, 23 January 1970, pp. 450–3.

[2] Cf. R. Ruether, "Post-Ecumenical Christianity", *The Ecumenist*, 5 (Nov.–Dec. 1966), pp. 3–7.

no longer feel at home in the churches of their origin. In their eyes, these churches are today mainly concerned with the defence of their own institutions and privileges, and neglect the burning social and political problems of the world. While these Christians are often isolated and exposed to great loneliness, they form friendships rather spontaneously when they do meet and remain together as a new fellowship. They have passed through the same transformation. They speak the same language. They are united in Christ in a manner that transcends the inherited ecclesiastical boundaries yet permits them to remain faithful to their past. We find such Christian groups around universities and colleges, around some Christian centres, retreat houses, book stores, adult education centres, etc.; we find them gathering around gifted lay people who are articulate and exercise Christian leadership. These Christians are still—nobody knows how long—the loyal men and women who give Christian witness in the present social crisis, who are exploring the inner life, and who follow the theological developments in the churches. These people were created by the same socio-spiritual development that produced the exodus from the priesthood. They and the priests of the free ministry belong together. They are the people to whom the ministry of the SPFM is directed. Here these priests have their communities.

Is the free ministry a valid concept? In a letter written by the Roman Congregation *Pro Doctrina Fidei* to Bishop F. L. Begin of Oakland, California, the free ministry is condemned as inauthentic: it is based on an erroneous understanding of the Catholic priesthood. The authors of this letter probably regard the canonical link to the apostolic hierarchy as an essential mark of the Catholic priesthood. Since theologians have come to recognize the charismatic and exceptional in the divine dispensation regarding the Church, there seems to be room for more positive evaluations of the free ministry.

More positive theological reflections on the free ministry and its place in the Church have been proposed at the annual conventions of the SPFM, and are available in the proceedings of these meetings. Eugene Bianchi, the President of the SPFM, has written an ecclesiological essay on the free ministry;[3] Rocco

[3] *Proceedings of the First Annual Convention* (1969), pp. 3-16.

Caporale has given a socio-religious justification and explanation of the free ministry;[4] Bernard Cooke, James Megivern and Gregory Baum have explored the theological significance of the free ministry.[5] These authors assume that something significant is changing in the Catholic Church; that we are moving towards greater pluriformity within Catholicism; that this transition takes place at different speeds in various groups in the Church; and that for these reasons the uniform categories of the past are no longer adequate for the evaluation of present developments. There is room, they think, for a free ministry in the Church.

Opposed to this view is George Tavard, noted theologian and historian. In an editorial in the *Journal of Ecumenical Studies*,[6] he compares the priests advocating a free ministry with the *episcopi vagantes* in the Anglican Church. These men had sought episcopal consecration outside their own church, from Orthodox or Old Catholic bishops, and then returned to their church in search of an episcopal role. They were indeed clerics without a people, and as such they were not recognized by the Anglican Church. Similarly, for Tavard, the priests advocating a free ministry are clerics without a people; they have no place in the Church. Gregory Baum replied to Tavard in the same journal.[7] He tried to show that the analogy between the *episcopi vagantes* and the SPFM does not hold. The priests of the free ministry are surrounded by a community of Christians, produced by the identical socio-spiritual development. They offer a valid service, a legitimate ministry. One may hope that a sustained conversation with the institutional Church will eventually lead to an acknowledgment of pluriformity in the ministry. Unity in ministry cannot be identified with the uniformity of the law.

For the time being, the problem perdures. Whether the SPFM survives is not the issue. Since the number of priests leaving the official ministry continues to grow, the problem is intensified. The message implicit in this ecclesiastical development is only

---

[4] *Proceedings of the Second Annual Convention* (1970), pp. 37–49.
[5] *Proceedings of the Third Annual Convention* (1971).
[6] 7 (1970), pp. 777–9.
[7] 8 (1971), pp. 344–9.

too clear. It is high time that the U.S. hierarchy recognized that a significant section of ardent and committed Christians are moving to the margin of the institution, not because they are attracted by what the Scriptures call the "world", but because in their eyes the hierarchy has embraced a worldly view of law and authority, and a worldly desire to please those who are powerful in the nation.

Biographical Notes

JEAN-JACQUES VON ALLMEN was born in Lausanne in 1917 and ordained pastor in the Reformed Church in 1941. He studied in Lausanne, Basle and Neuchâtel. Doctor of theology, he is professor of practical theology at the Faculty of Theology of the University of Neuchâtel. He is also research counsellor in the "Faith and Constitution" section of the Ecumenical Council of the Churches. Among his published works are: *Prophétisme sacramentel* (Neuchâtel, 1964), *Essai sur le repas du Seigneur* (Neuchâtel, 1966) and *Le saint ministère selon la conviction et la volonté des réformes du XVIe siècle* (Neuchâtel, 1968).

GREGORY BAUM, O.S.A., was born 20 June 1923 in Berlin and ordained in 1954. He studied at the University of Fribourg, at McMaster University, Hamilton (Canada) and at Ohio State University. Doctor of theology, and doctor (h.c.) of three universities, he is professor of theology at St Michael's College, University of Toronto. He is also editor of *The Ecumenist*. Among his published works are: *Faith and Doctrine* (1969) and *Man Becoming* (1970).

BORIS BOBRINSKOY was born 15 February 1925 in Paris and ordained in the Orthodox Church in 1959. He is professor of dogmatic theology at the Saint-Serge Institute of Orthodox Theology and at the Higher Institute of Ecumenical Studies, Paris. He is also rector of the French Orthodox parish, Paris, and a member of the "Faith and Constitution" Commission of the Ecumenical Council of the Churches. Among his published works are contributions to *Des chrétiens s'interrogent sur l'Intercommunion* (Paris, 1969) and *Le Baptême* (Paris, 1971).

WALTER KASPER was born 3 March 1933 in Heidenheim (Germany) and ordained in 1957. He studied at the Universities of Tübingen and Munich. Doctor of theology, he is a professor at the Seminary of Catholic Theology (University of Tübingen). Among his published works are: *Das Absolute in der Geschichte: Philosophie und Theologie der Geschichte in der Spätphilosophie Schellings* (Mainz, 1965) and *Dogma unter dem Wort Gottes* (Mainz, 1965).

ULRICH KÜHN was born 16 March 1932 in Halle/Saale (Germany). He studied Evangelical theology at the Karl-Marx University of Leipzig. Doctor of systematic theology, he is lecturer in systematic theology at the Seminary of Theology, Leipzig. He is also president of the Leiter der Konfessionskundlichen Forschungstelle of the Federation of Evangelical Churches, East Germany, and a member of the Commission for Faith and Ecclesial Order. Among his published works is *Via caritatis. Theologie des Gesetzes bei Thomas von Aquin* (Berlin, 1965).

HERVÉ-MARIE LEGRAND, O.P., was born 15 October 1935 in France and ordained in 1963. He studied at the Faculties of the Saulchoir, at Walberberg (Germany) and at the Universities of St Thomas (Rome), Strasbourg and Athens. Licentiate of philosophy and doctor of theology, he teaches at the Faculty of Theology of the Saulchoir. Among his published works are contributions to *La charge pastorale des évêques* (Unam Sanctam 74) (Paris, 1969) and *Pour une théologie du ministère* (Gembloux/Paris, 1971).

Jos LESCRAUWAET, M.S.C., was born 19 June 1923 in Amsterdam and ordained in 1948. He studied at the University of Nijmegen. Doctor of theology he is professor of dogmatic theology at the Faculty of Theology, Tilburg (Netherlands). He is a member of the International Theological Commission and of the Joint Commission of the Roman Catholic Church and the World Alliance of Presbyterian Churches. Among his published works are: *De Bijbel over de christelijke eenheid* (1961), *Compendium van het Oecumenisme* (1962) and *Einheit der Ökumene* (1969).

FRANKLIN LITTELL was born 20 June 1917 in Syracuse (U.S.A.) and ordained in the Methodist Church in 1941. He studied at Cornell College, Union Theological Seminary and at Yale University. Master of arts, doctor of theology, doctor (h.c.) of the University of Marburg, he is professor of religion at Temple University, Philadelphia. Among his published works are: *The Anabaptist View of the Church* ([2]1958) and *The Origins of Sectarian Protestantism* ([2]1964).

PETER VAN LEEUWEN, O.F.M., was born 6 April 1913 in Leerdam (Netherlands) and ordained in 1938. He studied at the Universities of Louvain and Nijmegen. Doctor of theology, he is professor of systematic theology at the University of Nijmegen. He was an expert at the Second Vatican Council. He has written articles on fundamental theology, the structure of the Church, ecumenism and mixed marriages.

JOHN McKENZIE was born 9 October 1910 in Brazil, Indiana, and ordained in 1939. He studied at St Louis University, at St Mary's College (Kansas) and at Weston College. Master of arts and doctor of theology he is professor of the Old Testament at De Paul University (Chicago). Among his published works are: *Authority in the Church* (1966) and *The Roman Catholic Church* (1969).

JOHN MACQUARRIE was born 27 June 1919 in Renfrew and ordained in the Anglican Church in 1965. He studied at Glasgow University, gaining degrees in arts, philosophy and theology. He has been professor of systematic theology at Union Theological Seminary, New York, since 1962. His published works include *God and Secularity* (1967) and *Martin Heidegger* (1968).

HARRY McSORLEY was born 20 December 1931 in Philadelphia. He studied in the U.S.A. at Bucknell University and St Paul's College, Washington, and in Germany at Paderborn, Heidelberg, Tübingen and Munich. Master of arts and doctor of theology, he is professor of theology at Toronto

University. Among his publications are *Luther: Right or Wrong* (New York, 1969) and *The Infallibility Debate* (New York, 1971).

HARDING MEYER was born 19 January 1928 in Hardingen (Germany) and is a Lutheran Evangelical. Doctor of theology, he is professor of research at the Institute of Ecumenical Research, Strasbourg. Among his published works are: *Pascals Pensées als dialogische Verkündigung* (1962) and *Das Wort Pius IX: Die Tradition bin ich* (1965).

ALBERT OUTLER was born 17 November 1908 in Thomasville (U.S.A.) and ordained in the Methodist Church in 1931. He studied at Emory and Yale Universities. Doctor of philosophy, he is professor of theology at the Perkins School of Theology, Southern Methodist University, Dallas. He is also President-Elect of the American Catholic Historical Association. Among his published works are: *Psychotherapy and the Christian Message* (1954) and *Who Trusts in God?: Musings on the Meaning of Providence*.

HÉBERT ROUX was born 16 May 1902 in Montauban and ordained in the Reformed Church of France in 1928. He studied at the Universities of Bordeaux and Paris and at the Faculties of Protestant Theology in Montpellier and Paris. Licentiate of philosophy and theology, doctor (h.c.) of theology, he is co-president of the Joint Catholic-Protestant Committee of France. He was a delegated observer at Vatican II. Among his published works are: *Le Concile et le Dialogue Oecuménique* (Paris, 1964) and *Détresse et promesse de Vatican II* (Paris, 1967).

HERBERT RYAN, s.j., was born in 1931 in New York and ordained in 1962. He studied at the Gregorian University, Rome, gaining a doctorate in theology. He is associate professor of historical theology at Woodstock College, New York. He is also a member of the Commissions (American and International) on relations between the Anglican Church and the Catholic Church.

MASSEY SHEPERD is a minister of the Episcopal Church of the U.S.A. Doctor of philosophy and of theology, he is professor of liturgy at the Church Divinity School of the Pacific at Berkeley. He was an Anglican observer at the third session of Vatican II and a member of the Anglican-Roman Catholic Joint Preparatory Commission.

MAURICE VILLAIN, s.m., was born 16 May 1900 in Argenton (France) and ordained in 1927. Doctor of theology, he has been a professor at the Ecumenical Institute, Bossey (Switzerland), at the Higher Institute of Ecumenical Studies, Paris, and at the Universities of Montreal, Buenos Aires and Warsaw. Among his published works are: *Introduction à l'Oecuménisme* (Paris, ⁴1964), *Vatican II et le dialogue oecuménique* (Paris, 1966) and *La prière oecuménique* (Paris/Montreal, 1970). He contributes an ecumenical column to *Rythmes du Monde* and to *Figaro*.

JOHN ZIZIOULAS was born in 1931 in Greece. He studied at the Universities of Salonica and Athens and also at Harvard University. Doctor of theology (Harvard) and of Orthodox theology (Athens) he is professor of patristic theology at Edinburgh University. Among his publications are "The Unity of the Church in the Eucharist and the Bishop during the First Three Centuries" (in Greek), and many articles on ecclesiology and the Eucharist.